# *Seabrook's*

# *Antique Shop*

# *Guide*

## Covering over 2200 shops

### in

# Southeastern Pennsylvania
# New Jersey & Delaware

The only comprehensive county by county
directory to the antique shops of the tri-state area.

## 1ST Edition

A publication of Seabrook Scott Trading Company
West Chester, Pennsylvania

ISBN: 0-9661677-0-8

**Attention: This guide is available at quantity discounts for educational, resale, fundraising, sales and promotional uses.**

Please contact:

Seabrook Scott Trading Company, 1512 West Chester Pike, #174,
West Chester, PA 19382
Phone: (610) 722-0919
Fax: (610) 722-0440

381
SEA

Printed and bound in the United States of America.

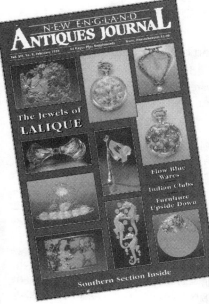

3

# ORDER FORM

To order additional copies of

## Seabrook's Antique Shop Guide

Call: (610) 722-0919
Fax: (610) 722-0440

Or

Photocopy this page and send check or money order to:

Seabrook Scott Trading Company
1512 West Chester Pike, #174
West Chester, PA 19382

Name: _____

Address: _____

City: _____

State: _____

Zip: _____

Phone: _____

Enclosed please find my check or money order for (check one):

☐ 1 Book  $13.95 + $ 3.95 (Shipping & Handling & 6% PA tax) = $17.90
☐ 2 Books $27.90 + $ 7.90 (Shipping & Handling & 6% PA tax) = $35.80
☐ 3 Books $41.85 + $11.85 (Shipping & Handling & 6% PA tax) = $53.70
☐ 4 Books $55.80 + $15.80 (Shipping & Handling & 6% PA tax) = $71.60

Please allow 6-8 weeks for delivery.

# Attention Shops & Shoppers!

Contact us regarding: new shops, shop location changes or new hot spots.

Call us, (610) 722-0919
Fax us, (610) 722-0440 or

Send us:
Seabrook Scott Trading Company
1512 West Chester Pike, #174
West Chester, PA 19382

Provide the following information:

Shop Name: _____

Address: _____

City: State: Zip: _____

Phone: _____

Description or Shop specialty_____

# Contents

8

11

# Introduction

Dear Readers:

Welcome to the first edition of Seabrook's Antique Shop Guide, the only comprehensive resource for antique shops in Southeastern Pennsylvania, New Jersey, and Delaware.

Used by the both novice and the experienced collector to locate shops throughout the tri-state area that carry antique, unique and older items, this book lists over 2,200 resources for antiques including: antique shops, antique co-ops, antiquarian booksellers, auction houses, flea markets and thrift shops.

Arranged geographically and alphabetically, this book is composed of three main sections: Pennsylvania, New Jersey and Delaware. The three main sections are then further divided into the counties within each state and then by the towns within each county. The antique dealers are listed alphabetically under their respective states, counties and towns. This format provides a "snapshot" of the shops in each geographic area, enabling the traveler, local or out of town, to view the shops in each area and choose their destinations (and convenient stops along the way).

Our goal is to present the reader with the most complete, comprehensive and factual information. Because of this commitment to quality, quantity and integrity, the shops presented in this directory were thoroughly researched but not "rated". The task of "rating" or evaluating a shop is a matter of opinion and each individual collector can and will make their own judgements based upon his or her budget and needs.

The nature of the antiques business dictates varied and or seasonal hours. Therefore, we do recommend that you call several shops to get their hours prior to planning day or weekend visits. We also recommend that you shop often, inventory changes frequently.

In the process of exploring each area, you may find yourself picking through thrift shops, experiencing the thrill of the auction bidding process, quietly viewing fine antiques in a gallery setting, or drawing inspiration from tastefully decorated boutique-style shops. All are part of the excitement of searching and collecting and you will find precisely this mix of shop styles as you investigate each area. Also, as you peruse each section, we are confident that you will be surprised to notice many previously undiscovered shops and unknown "hot spots" within your town and surrounding areas.

Collecting can not only become a method for changing your environment and decorating your home but also a medium for increasing your knowledge about antiques and history, refining your tastes, enhancing your skills and developing your personal style.

We appreciate your feedback, positive or negative, and look forward to hearing from you. Contact us at (610) 722-0919.

Happy Hunting.

# Delaware

**Kent County**
**New Castle County**
**Sussex County**

# Kent County

**Dover**
**Felton**
**Hartley**
**Leipsic**
**Smyrna**

# Dover

Ancestor's Antiques
4004C S. Dupont Hwy. (Rt. 13)
Dover, DE
(302) 698-0600

Carol's Collectibles
N. Dupont Hwy. (Rt. 13)
Dover, DE
NO Phone

Dover Antique Mart
4621 Dupont Highway (Rt. 13)
Dover, DE
(302) 734-7844

Harmic's Antiques Gallery
Bishop's Corner & Dupont Hwy.
 (Rt. 13)
Dover, DE
(302) 736-1174

Heart Strings
136 W. Loockerman St.
Dover, DE
(302) 674-9016

James M. Kilvington Antiques
103 N. Bradford
Dover, DE
(302) 734-9124
(By appointment)

Paul's Antiques & Furniture
4304 N. Dupont Hwy. (Rt.13)
Dover, DE
(302) 734-2280

Robert's Antique Lamps
2035 S. Dupont Hwy. (Rt.13)
Dover, DE
(302) 697-3414

Spence's Auction, Farmer's & Flea
 Market
550 S. New St.
Dover, DE
(302) 734-3441
(Auctions every Tues & Fri, 8:00am.)

Sweet Memories Antiques &
 Collectibles
5084 N. Dupont Hwy. (Rt. 13)
Dover, DE
(302) 736-3533

# Felton

Canterbury Used Furniture & Antiques
On Rt. 13 at intersection of Routes 13 & 15
8 miles South of Dover on Rt. 13
Felton, DE
(302) 284-9567

# Hartley

L.G. Antiques
Rt. 44 and Judith Rd.
Hartly, DE
(302) 492-8791

# Leipsic

Old Leipsic Antiques
Main St.
Leipsic, DE
(302) 736-0595
(By Appointment)

# Smyrna

A Bit of the Past Antiques
3511 S. Dupont Hwy. (Rt. 13)
Smyrna, DE
(302) 653-9963

Attic Treasures
2119 S. Dupont Hwy. (Rt. 13)
Smyrna, DE
(302) 653-6566/653-9520

C & J Antiques
5767 Dupont Hwy. (Rt. 13)
Smyna, DE
(302) 653-4903

Duck Creek Antiques
5756 N. DuPont Hwy. (Rt. 13)
Smyrna, DE
(302) 653-8396
(Appointment only)

Eileen Gant Antiques
5527 N. Dupont Hwy. (Rt. 13)
Smyrna, DE
(302) 653-6229/653-8996

Out Back Antiques
Rt. 13 (Southbound)
Smyrna, DE
(302) 653-7807

The Tin Sedan
12 N. Main St.
Smyrna, DE
(302) 653-3535

The What Nott Shop
5786 N. Dupont Hwy.
Smyrna, DE
(302) 653-3855

Smyrna Antiques
3114 S. Dupont Hwy. (Rt. 13)
(2 miles South of Smyrna)
Smyrna, DE
(302) 659-0373

Sono Antiquarian
Smyrna, DE
(302) 653-5044
(By appointment only.)

# New Castle County

Bear
Bellefonte
Centreville
Claymont
Delaware City
Elsmere
Greenville
Hayden Park
Hockessin
Hollyoak
Middletown
New Castle
Newark
Newport
Stanton
Wilmington
Yorklyn

# Bear

Carter's Used Furniture
1880 Pulaski Highway (Rt. 40)
Bear, DE
(302) 834-1075

# Bellefonte

Bellefonte Shoppe
901 Brandywine Blvd.
Bellefonte, DE
(302) 764-0637

Brandywine Resale Shop
900 Brandywine Blvd.
Bellefonte, DE
(302) 764-4544

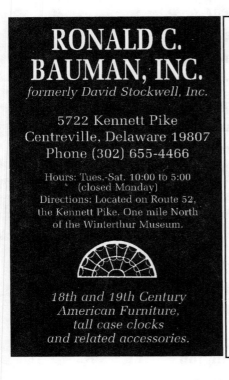

# Centreville

Barbara'a Antiques & Books
5900 Kennett Pike
Centreville, DE
(302) 655-3055

Centreville Antiques
5716 Kennett Pike
Centreville, DE
(302) 571-0771

Jackson-Mitchell Inc
5718 Kennett Pike
Centreville, De
(302) 656-0110

Ronald Bauman Inc.
5722 Kennett Pike
Centreville, DE
(302) 655-4466

# Centreville (continued)

The Resettlers Galleries
5801 Kennett Pike
Centreville, DE
(302) 658-9097

Twice Nice Antiques & Collectibles
Frederick's Country Center
5714 Kennett Pike
Centerville, DE
(302) 656-8881

Windle & Malchione Antiques
Frederick Country Center
Kennett Pike (Rt. 52)
Centreville, DE
(302) 651-9222

# Claymont

A A A Claymont Antiques
2811 Philadelphia Pike
Claymont, DE
(302) 798-1771

Lamb's Loft
16 Commonwealth Ave.
Claymont, DE
(302) 792-9620
(over 50 dealers)

The Glass Porch
2201 Philadelphia Pike
Claymont, DE
(302) 798-5261
(By Appointment)

Trescott Haines
2811 Philadelphia Pike
Claymont, DE
(302) 475-8398
(By appointment only)

# Delaware City

The Old Canal Shops
129 Clinton
Delaware City, DE
(302) 834-5262

# Elsmere

Merrill's Antiques
100 Northern Ave.
Elsmere, DE
(302) 994-1765

# Greenville

Products of Great Import
Greenville Shopping Center
Rt. 52
Greenville, DE
(302) 654-5075
(Rugs)

The Furniture Exchange Ltd.
Greenville Crossing II
4001 Kennett Pike
Greenville, DE
(302) 658-1414

# Hayden Park

Doyle's Antiques & Gifts
601 S. Maryland Ave.
Hayden Park, DE
(302) 994-1424

# Hockessin

Accents Art & Antiques
1304C Old Lancaster Pike
Hockessin, DE
(302) 235-1766

Alleman & Company
500 Hockessin Corner
Hockessin, DE
(302) 234-9872

# Hollyoak

Browse & Buy
1704 Philadelphia Pike
Hollyoak, DE
(302) 798-5866

Red Barn Shoppes
400 Silverside Rd.
Hollyoak, DE
(302) 792-0555

Holly Oak Corner Store
1600 Philadelphia Pike
Hollyoak, DE
(302) 798-0255
(By Appointment)

# Middletown

Butler & Cook Antiques
13 E. Main St.
Middletown, DE
(302) 378-7022

G.W. Thomas Antiques
2496 Dupont Parkway (Rt. 13)
Middletown, DE
(302) 378-2414

Daniel Bennett Shutt Inc.
123 W. Main St.
Middletown, DE
(302) 378-0890

MacDonough Antique Center
2501 Dupont Parkway (Rt.13)
Middletown, DE
(302) 378-0485/378-0176/888-635-4529

# New Castle

Cobblestones
406 Delaware St.
New Castle, DE
(302) 322-5088

The Raven's Nest
204 Delaware St.
New Castle, DE
(302) 325-2510

Lauren Lynch
1 East Second St.
New Castle, DE
(302) 328-5576

Yesterday's Rose
204 Delaware St.
New Castle, DE
(302) 322-3001

Opera House Antiques Center
308 Delaware St.
New Castle, DE
(302) 326-1211

# Newark

Chapel Street Antiques
197 S. Chapel St.
Newark, DE
(302) 366-0700

Main Street Antiques
280 E. Main St.
Newark, DE
(302) 733-7677
(16 dealers)

# Newark (continued)

Old Tyme Antiques
294 E. Main St.
Newark, DE
(302) 366-8411

Yesterday's Treasures
2860 Ogletown Rd. (Rt. 273)
Newark, DE
(302) 292-8362

## Newport

The Grey Parrot
13 W. Market St.
Newport, DE
(302) 999-9609

## Stanton

Impulse Antiques
216 E. Main St.
Stanton, DE
(302) 994-7737

Shatley's
415 Main St.
Stanton, DE
(302) 994-7052

# Wilmington

Antique & Not So
24-A Trolley Square
Wilmington, DE
(302) 656-3011

Grandma's Treasures Inc.
1709 Philadelphia Pike
Wilmington, DE
(302) 792-2820

Better Homes & Bargains
401 Philadelphia Pike
Wilmington, DE
(302) 764-3777

Jung's Oriental Antiques & Fine Arts
1314 W. 13 St.
Wilmington, DE
(302) 658-1314

Brandywine Trading Company
804 Brandywine Blvd.
Wilmington, DE
(302) 761-9175

LaFemme Mystique Boutique
Trolley Square Shopping Center
Gilpin & Delaware Ave.
Wilmington, DE
(302) 651-9331

Brandywine Treasure Shop
1913 N. Market St.
Wilmington, DE
(302) 656-4464

Reeves Used Furniture
4821 Governor Printz Blvd.
Wilmington, DE
(302) 764-5582

Catholic Thrift Center
1320 E. 23rd St.
Wilmington, DE
(302) 764-2717

The Resettlers Annex
1005 W. 27th St.
Wilmington, DE
(302) 654-8255

F. H. Herman Antiques
308 Philadelphia Pike
Wilmington, DE
(302) 764-5333

The Red Barn Shoppes
400 Silverside Rd.
Wilmington, DE
(302) 792-0555

Golden Eagle Shop
1905 N. Market St.
Wilmington, DE
(302) 651-3460

The Willow Tree
1605 E. Newport Pike
  (Maryland Ave.)
Wilmington, DE
(302) 998-9004

Vintage Records
604 N. Market St. Mall
Wilmington, DE
(302) 656-2444
(records)

Wright's Antiques
702 W. Newport Pike
Wilmington, DE
(302) 994-3002

# Yorklyn

A Touch of the Orient
Garrett Snuff Mills (Intersection of
  Rt. 82 & Yorklyn Rd.)
Yorklyn, DE
(302) 239-4636

# Sussex County

Bethany Beach
Bridgeville
Clarksville
Coolspring
Dagsboro
Delmar
Ellendale
Fenwick Island
Georgetown
Greenwood
Gumboro
Harbeson
Laurel
Lewes
Milford
Milton
Millsboro
Millville
Ocean View
Rehoboth Beach
Seaford
Selbyville

# Bethany Beach

Beach Plum Antiques
Fifth & Pennsylvania Ave.
Bethany Beach, DE
(302) 539-6677

# Bridgeville

Affordably Yours of Bridgeville
Rt. 404 (1/4 mi. W. of Rt. 13)
Bridgeville, DE
(302) 337-9747

The Bridgeville Emporium
105 Market St.
Bridgeville, DE
(302) 337-7663

Antique Alley
Rt 13 (Southbound)
Bridgeville, DE
(800) 848-8277/(302)337-3137
(20 dealers)

The Menagerie
113 Market St.
Bridgeville, DE
(302) 337-7766

Pioneer Antiques
111 Market St.
Bridgeville, DE
(302) 337-3665

# Clarksville

Cranberry House Antiques
Rt. 26 (westbound) & Rd. 346
Clarksville, DE
(302) 934-8643

The Browsery
Rt. 26
Clarksville, DE
(302) 537-1505

Hudson's General Store
Corner Rt. 26 (westbound) & Rd. 348
Clarksville, DE
(302) 539-8709/(302) 539-5605

# Coolspring

York's Homestead Antiques
Lewes-Georgetown Hwy. (Rt. 9)
Coolspring, DE
(302) 684-3262

# Dagsboro

Becky's Country Gift Barn
400 Clayton St. (Rt. 26)
Dagsboro, DE
(302) 732-1314

Red Rooster
503 Main St. (Rt. 26)
Dagsboro, DE
(302) 732-1088

# Delmar

Delmar Household Consignment
  Center
Rt. 13A
Delmar, DE
(302) 846-3598

Joy's Antique Barn
610 N. 2nd St.
Delmar, DE
(302) 846-3671

# Ellendale

Collector's Exchange
Rt. 113 (northbound)
Ellendale, DE
(302) 422-2255

# Fenwick Island

Route 54 Antiques Complex
Rt. 54 (6 mi. East of Fenwick)
Fenwick Island, DE
(302) 436-5189

Seaside Country Store
Rt. 1 (southbound)
Fenwick Island, DE
(302) 539-6110

Seaport Antique Village Inc.
Rt. 54 (westbound) at the bridge
Fenwick Island, DE
(302) 436-8962

# Georgetown

Candlelight Antiques
406 N. Dupont Hwy.
(Rt. 113-northbound)
Georgetown, DE
(302) 856-7880

Morgan's Antiques, Crafts &
  Collectibles
134 East Market St.
  (Rt. 9-Eastbound)
Georgetown, DE
(302) 856-9147

Collectors Corner & Pawn Shop
101 E. Market St.
Georgetown, DE
(302) 856-7006

Passwater's Antiques
1028 E. Market St. (Rt. 9-Eastbound)
Georgetown, DE
(302) 856-6667

Georgetown Antiques Market
105 E. Market St.
(One block East of the Circle)
Georgetown, DE
(302) 856-7118

Signs of the Past Antiques
Rt. 9 (westbound)
3 1/2 mi. East of Georgetown circle
Georgetown, DE
(302) 856-9189

Generations Antiques
Rt. 9 (Westbound)
(3 miles East of Georgetown)
Georgetown, DE
(302) 856-6750

The Gas Station Antiques
546 N. Dupont Hwy.
Georgetown, DE
(302) 855-1127

Market Street Antiques & Collectibles
Rt. 9
Georgetown, DE
(302) 856-9006
(20 Dealers)

# Greenwood

Greenwood Antiques
Rt. 16 (Eastbound)
Greenwood, DE
(302) 349-5656

Hilltop Station
Rt. 13 South & 16 West
Greenwood, DE
(302) 349-9080

Obier's Antiques
Rt. 13 (N. of Greenwood)
Greenwood, DE
(302) 349-4694

Ruth Mervine Antiques
Rt. 36 (approx. 1 mi. N. of Rt. 16)
Greenwood, DE
(302) 349-4282

The Pine Cupboard
Rt. 16 (westbound)
Greenwood, DE
(302) 349-5150

# Gumboro

Cross Country Antiques & Crafts
Intersection of Rts. 26 & 54
Gumboro, DE
(302) 238-0129

Memory Lane
Rt. 26 (westbound)
Gumboro, DE
(302) 238-0100/ 238-7435

# Harbeson

Brick Barn Antiques
Rt. 9 (eastbound)
Harbeson, DE
(302) 684-4442
(Open May 1-Dec 22.)

Pete's Antiques
Rt. 9
Harbeson, DE
(302) 684-8188

# Laurel

Adam's Antiques
400 E. Sixth St.
Laurel, DE
(302) 875-9010

Bargain Bill's Flea Market
Rts. 13 & 9 (S.E. corner)
Laurel, DE
(302) 875-9958/875-2478

Bargain Carnival
310 N. Central Ave.
(On alternate Rt. 13 )
Laurel, DE
(302) 875-1662

Delmarva Antiques
Rt. 13 (northbound)
Laurel, DE
(302) 875-2200

Melvin L. Arion
635 E. 4th St.
Laurel, DE
(302) 875-5326
(By Appointment)

Oak Haven Antiques
S. Central Ave. (Extended)
Rt. 13A
Laurel, DE
(302) 875-3591

O'Neal's Antiques
Rt. 13 & 466
Laurel, DE
(302) 875-3391

Spring Garden Antiques
Delaware Ave. (Extended)
Laurel, DE
(302) 875-7015
(By Appointment)

The Golden Door
214 E. Market St.
Laurel, DE
(302) 875-5084

The Laurel Trading Company
206 Delaware Ave.
Laurel, DE
(302) 875-1770

This & That Used Furniture &
Antiques
Rt. 13
Laurel, DE
(302) 875-9760

Wells Lamp Studio
Rt. 13 (northbound)
Laurel, DE
(302) 875-5611

## Lewes

Auntie M's Emporium
116 West 3rd St.
Lewes, DE
(302) 644-1804

Auntie M's Emporium
203 B Second St.
Lewes, DE
(302) 644-2242

Antique Corner
142 Second St.
Lewes, DE
(302) 645-7233

Antique Village (at Red Mill)
221 Rt. 1 (Northbound)
Lewes, DE
(302) 645-1940

Antique Village Mall
221 Hwy. 1
Lewes, DE
(302) 644-0842

Beaman's Old & Gnu Antiques
Rt. 1 (Northbound)
Lewes, DE
(302) 645-8080

Classic Country Antiques
3.5 miles West of Rt. 1 on Rt. 9
   (Georgetown-Lewes Hwy.)
Lewes, DE
(302) 684-3285

Copper Penny Antiques
109 Market St.
Lewes, DE
(302) 645-2983

Feedmill Finds Antiques
New Rd. and U.S. Rt. 1
U.S. Rt. 1
Lewes, DE
(302) 645-1640

Garage Sale Antiques
1416 Rt. 1 (southbound)
Lewes, DE
(302) 645-1205

G.C. Vernon Fine Art
1566 Rt. 1
Lewes, DE
(302) 645-7905

Heritage Antique Mall
130 Hwy. 1
Lewes, DE
(302) 645-2309 / 645-8957

Jewell's Antiques & Jewelry
118 Second St.
Lewes, DE
(302) 645-1828

Lewes Mercantile Antique
Gallery
109 Second St.
Lewes, DE
(302) 645-7900

Practically Yours
Rt. 9
Lewes, DE
(302) 684-8936
(30 dealers)

Queen Anne's Railroad
King's Hwy.
Lewes, DE
(302) 644-1726

The Swan's Nest
107 Kings Hwy.
Lewes, DE
(302) 645-8403

The Pack Rat
1165 Rt. 1 (northbound)
Lewes, DE
(302) 645-5277

Then And Now Antiques
1552 Savannah Rd.
   (Eastbound Rt. 9)
Lewes, DE
(302) 645-9821

Thistles
203 Second St.
Lewes, DE
(302) 644-2323

## Milford

Bean Furniture & Antique Shop
614 N. W. Front St.
Milford, DE
(302) 422-4936

War Relics Shop
RD1
Milford, DE
(302) 422-5487

## Milton

Jail House Antiques
106 Union St.
Milton, DE
(302) 684-8660

Vern's Used Furniture
128 Broad St.
Milton, DE
(302) 684-4642

The Riverwalk Shoppe
Milton Complex
105 Union St.
Milton, DE
(302) 684-1500

## Millsboro

Antique Alley
225 Main St.
Millsboro, DE
(302) 934-9841

Millsboro Bazaar
238 Main St.
Millsboro, DE
(302) 934-7413

Antique Bouquet
201 N. Dupont Hwy.
(Rt. 113-northbound)
Millsboro, DE
(302) 934-9175

Parson's Antiques
Rt. 24 (Eastbound)
Millsboro, DE
(302) 934-6008

Antique Mall of Millsboro
401 Dupont Hwy.
(Rt.113-norhtbound)
Millsboro, DE
(302) 934-1915
(over 40 dealers)

The Consignery
201 Washington St. (Rt. 54)
Millsboro, DE
(302) 934-8500

The Hudson House
Horseshoe Dr.
Millsboro, DE
(302) 934-6363
(By appointment only.)

Lynch's Antiques
320 Main St. (Eastbound)
Millsboro, DE
(302) 934-7217

# Millville

Great Expectations
Rt. 26
Millville, DE
(302) 537-6539
(multi-dealer shop)

Miller's Creek Antiques
Rt. 26 (westbound)
Millville, DE
(302) 539-4513

Ocean View Gift Gallery
Rt. 26 (Westbound)
Millville, DE
(302) 537-4003

Reflections Antiques
Rt. 26 (westbound)
At the Old Blue Church
Millville, DE
(302) 537-2308

# Ocean View

Antique Prints Ltd.
Central Ave. (Southbound)
2 blocks N. of Rt. 26
Ocean View, DE
(302) 539-6702

Cinnamon Owl Gifts & Antiques
Ocean View Center
Rt. 26 (westbound)
Ocean View, DE
(302) 539-1336

Echo Books, Etc.
Rt. 26
Ocean View, DE
(302) 537-1675

Heirloom Trunks
Cedar Neck Rd. (Rt. 357)
Ocean View, DE
(302) 539-8167

Iron Age Antiques
Central Ave. (Southbound)
Ocean View, DE
(302) 539-5344

Kennedy's Classics
Rt. 26 (1.5 mi. West on Rt. 1)
Ocean View, DE
(302) 537-5403

Out of the Blue/Georgette's -The
    Unusual Shop
Rt. 26 (Westbound)
Ocean View, DE
(302) 539-8843

White House Antiques & Gifts
Rt. 26 (behind the Cinnamon Owl)
Ocean View, DE
(May through Labor Day)

# Rehoboth Beach

Affordable Antique Mall
4300 Rt. 1
Rehoboth Beach, DE
(302) 227-5803

Early Attic
10 Sixth St.
Rehoboth Beach, DE
(302) 227-0598

Generations Antiques
New Rehoboth branch
237 Rehoboth Ave.
Rehoboth Beach, DE
(302) 227-2443

Stuart Kingston Incorporated
501 North Boardwalk (at Grenoble
    Place)
Rehoboth Beach, DE
(302) 227-2524

The Collector
237 Rehoboth Ave.
Rehoboth Beach, DE
(302) 227-1902

The Glass Flamingo
46 Baltimore Ave.
(Behind Something Special)
Rehoboth Beach, DE
(302) 226-1366

## Seaford

Seaford Antique Emporium
323 High St.
Seaford, DE
(302) 628-9111

Ann's Downtown Antiques
324 High St.
Seaford, DE
(302) 629-0430

Tea Tyme Antiques
Rt. 13 (north) and Tharpe Rd.
Seaford, DE
(302) 629-9313

## Selbyville

Ed & Ann's Antique Mall, Flea Market
&  Rag Tag Treasures
Rt. 54 (eastbound)
Selbyville, DE
(302) 436-9948

Sidetracked Antiques
Church St. & Railroad Ave.
Selbyville, DE
(302) 436-4488

# New Jersey

Atlantic County
Bergen County
Burlington County
Camden County
Cape May County
Cumberland County
Essex County
Gloucester County
Hudson County
Hunterdon County
Mercer County
Middlesex County
Monmouth County
Morris County
Ocean County
Passaic County
Salem County
Somerset County
Sussex County
Union County
Warren County

# Atlantic County

Absecon
Atlantic City
Egg Harbor
Hammonton
Margate
Mays Landing
Mizpah
Pleasantville
Scullville
Smithville
Somers Point
Ventnor
Weekstown
West Atlantic City

# Absecon

Cobweb Corner/Seascape Antiques
6th Ave. & White Horse Pike
Absecon, NJ
(609) 748-2522

The Chicken Coop Antique Shop
Pitney Rd. & Jimmy Leads Rd.
Absecon Highlands, NJ
(609) 652-9725

# Atlantic City

Antiquarium
Merv Griffin's Resorts
Atlantic City, NJ
(609) 340-6429
(Old books, Maps Prints)

Bayside Basin Antiques
800 N. New Hampshire Ave.
Atlantic City, NJ
(609) 347-7143
(By appt.)

Ed's Used Furniture & Antiques
915 Atlantic Ave.
Atlantic City, NJ
(609) 344-9758

Princeton Antiques Bookshop
2917 Atlantic Ave.
Atlantic City, NJ
(609) 344-1943
(Books & photographs, by
    appointment)

# Egg Harbor

Heinholdt Books
1325 W. Central Ave.
Egg Harbor, NJ
(609) 965-2284
(Books only, by appt.)

# Hammonton

Almost New Home Furnishings
133 Bellevue Ave. (Rt. 54)
Hammonton, NJ
(609) 704-9221

Arlene's Antiques & Collectibles
602 N. White Horse Pike
Hammonton, NJ
(609) 561-8410

Silver Plating of South Jersey
503 White Horse Pike
Hammonton, NJ
(609) 567-2239

# Margate

The Estate Sale
8001 Ventnor Ave.
Margate, NJ
(609) 823-3209

# Mays Landing

Gravelly Run Antiquarians
5045 Mays Landing Rd.
Mays Landing, NJ
(609) 625-7778
(Books only)

# Mizpah

The Potpourri Gallery
6953 Rt. 40 (Harding Hwy.)
Mizpah, NJ
(609) 476-2667

# Pleasantville

Consignment Galleries
10 E. Verona Ave. (Black Horse Pike)
Pleasantville, NJ
(609) 646-5353

Moni Mire Gift Attic
1008 S. New Rd.
Pleasantville, NJ
(609) 646-7841

Doc's Furniture Mart
881 Black Horse Pike
Pleasantville, NJ
(609) 641-5079

Mr. Joe's Hodge Podge Used Furniture
306 S. Main St.
Pleasantville, NJ
(609) 383-9833

# Scullville

The Red Garagee
1769 Rt. 559 (Mays Landing-Somers
    Point Rd.)
Scullville, NJ
(609) 653-0097

# Smithville

Country Folk
Rt. 9
Smithville, NJ
(609) 652-6161

Rose of Sharon Antiques & Collectibles
Village Green at Smithville
615 E. Moss Mill Rd.
Smithville, NJ
(609) 652-6300

# Somers Point

A Antiques & Estate Buyers
811-817 Shore Rd.
Somers Point, NJ
(609) 927-7897/927-9897

De Stefano Antiques
816 Shore Rd.
Somers Point, NJ
(609) 927-0848

Anything Collectible
812-B Shore Rd.
Somers Point, NJ
(609) 927-3809

Olde Bay Shoppe
Mays Landing Rd.
Somers Point, NJ
(609) 927-8081

# Ventnor

Antiques and More
6405 Ventnor Ave.
Ventnor City, NJ
(609) 823-8889

Black Bird Antiques
6510 Ventnor Ave.
Ventnor, NJ
(609) 823-0233

## Weekstown

Sawmill Antiques
2610 Back Rd.
Weekstown, NJ
(609) 965-2516

## West Atlantic City

Beacon Street Shops
7006 Black Horse Pike
West Atlantic City, NJ
(609) 646-9382

# Bergen County

Allendale
Bergenfield
Bogota
Cliffside Park
Closter
East Rutherford
Englewood
Fairview
Garfield
Glen Rock
Hackensack
Hillsdale
Ho Ho Kus
Lodi
Lyndhurst
Mahwah
Midland Park
Montvale
North Bergen
Norwood
Oakland
Oradel
Palisades
Paramus
Ramsay
Ridgewood
River Edge
Rutherford
Saddle River
Teaneck
Tenafly
Westwood
Wyckoff

## Allendale

Allendale Antiques
317 Franklin Tpk.
Allendale, NJ
(201) 825-2165

Now & Then
140 W. Allendale Ave.
Allendale, NJ
(201) 934-1440

## Bergenfield

Ambiance Antiques by
Larry A. Wenzel
79 N. Washington Ave.
Bergenfield, NJ
(201) 385-1111

Old Curiousity Shop
100 Portland Ave.
Bergenfield, NJ
(201) 387-7799
(Call for auction days & times.)

Antique Corner
50 W. Church St.
Bergenfield, NJ
(201) 384-8001

The Book Stop
52 S. Washington Ave.
Bergenfield, NJ
(201) 384-1162
(Books only)

# Bogota

Advalorem Books
14 E. Fort Lee Rd.
Bogota, NJ
(201) 525-1828
(Books only)

# Cliffside Park

Stan's Antiques
583 Anderson Ave.
Cliffside Park, NJ
(201) 945-4679

# Closter

Antique D'Zynes
70 Herbert Ave.
Closter, NJ
(201) 768-8844

Canterbury Mews Gallery
Closter Plaza
Closter, NJ
(201) 767-2300

# East Rutherford

American Coin Exchange
217 Patterson Ave.
E. Rutherford, NJ
(201) 933-2000

Charles P. Rogers Brass & Iron Beds
300 Rt. 17 N.
East Rutherford, NJ
(201) 933-8300

# Englewood

Antiques By Ophir Gallery
12 Palisade Park East
Englewood, NJ
(201) 871-0424

Bizet Antiques & Unusual Finds
6 S. Dean St.
Englewood, NJ
(201) 568-5345

Chelsea Square Inc.
10 Depot Square & Dean St.
Englewood, NJ
(201) 568-5911

Crown House Antiques
39 E. Palisade Ave.
Englewood, NJ
(201) 894-8789

Jewel Spiegel Galleries
30 N. Dean St.
Englewood, NJ
(201) 871-3577

Portobello Road Antiques
491 Grand Ave.
Englewood, NJ
(201) 568-5559

Rose Hill Auction Gallery
35 S. VanBrunt St.
Englewood, NJ
(201) 816-1940
(Call for auction dates & times.)

Royal Galleries Antiques
66 E. Palisade Ave.
Englewood, NJ
(201) 567-6354

Starr
1 Grand Ave.
Englewood, NJ
(201) 568-9090

The Book Store At Depot Square
8 S. Depot Square
Englewood, NJ
(201) 568-6563
(Books only)

The Curios Collector
473 Sylvan Ave.
Englewood Circle, NJ
(201) 568-3955

Tony Art Gallery
120 Grand Ave.
Englewood, NJ
(201) 568-7271

## Fairview

Art 'N Things By Sorrentino
133 Anderson Ave.
Fairview, NJ
(201) 943-2288
(toys)

## Garfield

Bedlam Brass Beds & Antiques
530 River Rd.
Garfield, NJ
(973) 546-5000

## Glen Rock

The Jewel Table
877 Prospect St.
Glen Rock, NJ
(201) 612-9027

## Hackensack

Grandma's Attic
23 Panta Place
Hackensack, NJ
(201) 487-0393

## Hillsdale

The Book Shop
430 Hillsdale Ave.
Hillsdale, NJ
(201) 391-9101
(Books only)

## Ho Ho Kus

Aviary Antiques
622 N. Maple Ave.
Ho Ho Kus, NJ
(201) 652-0002

Discovery Antiques
620 N. Maple Ave.
Ho Ho Kus, NJ
(201) 444-9170

Camelot Antiques
9 N Franklin Tpk.
Ho Ho Kus, NJ
(201) 444-5300

Regal Antiques LTD
181E. Franklin Tpk
Ho Ho Kus, NJ
(201) 447-5066

# Lodi

N. Richman & Associates
509 Westminister Place
Lodi, NJ
(973) 772-9027

# Lyndhurst

A & L Antiques & Collectibles
772 Riverside Ave.
Lyndhurst, NJ
(201) 438-0780

Stamps & Coins & Things
306 Valley Brook Ave.
Lyndhurst, NJ
(201) 933-4499

# Mahwah

Granny's Attic Antiques
142 Franklin Tpk.
Mahwah, NJ
(201) 529-5516

# Midland Park

Bergen Caning & Supply
230 Godwin Ave.
Midland Park, NJ
(201) 445-6888

The Blue Barn
60 Goffle Rd.
Midland Park, NJ
(201) 612-0227

Brownstone Mill Antique Center
11 Paterson Ave.
Midland Park, NJ
(201) 445-3074/ 652-9602
(20 dealers)

Time Will Tell
Godwin Plaza
644 Godwin Ave.
Midland Park, NJ
(201) 652-1025
(clocks)

GF Warhol & Company
18 Goffle Rd.
Midland Park, NJ
(201) 612-1010

Tuc-D-Away Antiques
229 Godwin Ave.
Midland Park, NJ
(201) 652-0730

# Montvale

The Marketplace
30 Chestnut Ridge Rd.
Montvale, NJ
(201) 391-3940
(7 dealers)

Montvale Antique Mall
30 Chestnut Ridge Rd.
Montvale, NJ
(201) 391-3940
(Over 15 dealers.)

# North Bergen

Park Antiques
9001 River Rd.
North Bergen, NJ
(201) 943-7828

# Norwood

Elsie Jenriche
505 Broadway
Norwood, NJ
(201) 768-1046

## Oakland

Summer Kitchen Antiques
3 Dogwood Dr. (Rt. 202)
Oakland, NJ
(201) 891-2997

Tilden Antiques
1 Pool Hollow Rd.
Oakland, NJ
(201) 405-0800

## Oradel

All American Antiques
650 Lotus Ave.
Oradel, NJ
(201) 599-2395

Pawprint Books
991 Phyllis Lane
Oradel, NJ
(201) 967-7306
(Books only, by appointment.)

## Palisades

Ado's Collectibles
271 11th Bergen Blvd.
Palisades Park, NJ
(201) 302-9684

## Paramus

Burton & LoveJoy Inc.
Rt. 4 East
Paramus, NJ
(201) 587-0030

Country Cottage Gifts
578 Paramus Rd.
Paramus, NJ
(201) 447-1122

## Ramsay

Golden Triangle Stamp & Coin
141 E. Main St.
Ramsay, NJ
(201) 825-3456

William Minery
259 Grove St.
Ramsay, NJ
(201) 825-8027

## Ridgewood

Beautiful Things From The Past
419 Goffle Rd.
Ridgewood, NJ
(201) 670-7090

Ivory Tower Inc.
38 Oak St.
Ridgewood, NJ
(201) 670-6191

Habitat Antiques
795 E. Glen Ave.
Ridgewood, NJ
(201) 447-2111
(By appointment.)

Ridgewood Furniture Refinishing
166 Chestnut St.
Ridgewood, NJ
(201) 652-5566

Hahn's Antiques
579 Goffle Rd.
Ridgewood, NJ
(201) 251-9444

Rug Gallery
16 Oak St.
Ridgewood, NJ
(201) 612-0900

Irish Eyes Imports
1 Cottage Place & E. Ridgewood St.
Ridgewood, NJ
(201) 445-8585

# River Edge

Brier Rose Books
26 River Edge Rd.
River Edge, NJ
(201) 967-1111
(Books only)

# Rutherford

Curio Shop
63 Park Ave.
Rutherford, NJ
(201) 531-9720

Morgan Marguerite Studio
6 Highland Cross
Rutherford, NJ
(201) 939-7222

# Saddle River

Carriage House Antiques
Barnstable Court
E. Allandale Rd.
Saddle River, NJ
(201) 327-2100

Yesterday's Treasures
7 Barnstable Court
Saddle River, NJ
(201) 825-1420

Richard C. Kyllo Antiques
210 W. Saddle River Rd.
Saddle River, NJ
(201) 327-7343

# Teaneck

Dason Lighting Inc.
1348 Teaneck Rd.
Teaneck, NJ
(201) 837-7831

Park Avenue Books
244 Park Ave.
Teaneck, NJ
(201) 836-0007
(Books only, by appt. or mail order.)

# Tenafly

A Gilded Cage
145 Dean Dr.
Tenafly, NJ
(201) 871-3002/445-9898

## Westwood

Bookwood Books
Box 263
Westwood, NJ
(201) 664-4066
(Books only, by appointment.)

Brass Towne
224 Fairview Ave.
Westwood, NJ
(201) 664-0167

Gardner's II Antiques
349 Broadway Ave.
Westwood, NJ
(201) 664-0612

The Treasure Cove
273 Westwood Ave.
Westwood, NJ
(201) 666-0054

Westwood Antiques
273 Westwood Ave.
Westwood, NJ
(201) 666-8988

## Wyckoff

Cheerful Heart
353 Franklin Ave.
Wyckoff, NJ
(201) 891-6991

L'Eglise
630 Wyckoff Ave.
Wyckoff, NJ
(201) 891-3622

# Burlington County

Bordentown
Burlington
Cinnaminson
Columbus
Crosswicks
Edgewater Park
Fort Dix
Hainesport
Mansfield
Maple Shade
Medford
Moorestown
Mount Holly
Mount Laurel
Pemberton
Rancocas
Riverside
Riverton
Vincentown

# Bordentown

Mark Reed Furniture Restoration &
   Conservation
102 Farnsworth Ave.
Bordentown, NJ
(609) 298-0716

Shoppe 202
202 Farnsworth Ave.
Bordentown, NJ
(609) 298-1424

# Burlington

Antique Row
307 High St.
Burlington, NJ
(609) 387-3050

Philip's Furniture
347 High St.
Burlington, NJ
(609) 386-7125/429-3869

H.G. Sharkey & Co.
306 High St.
Burlington, NJ
(609) 239-0200

Village Furniture Exchange
Burlington Center Mall
Rt. 541 & Bromley Blvd.
Burlington. NJ
(609) 387-7573

High Street Exchange
337 High St.
Burlington, NJ
(609) 239-3044

# Cinnaminson

River Road Antiques
1101 River Rd. (Broad St.)
Cinnaminson, NJ
(609) 829-0522

Vintage Village
1613 Cinnaminson Ave.
Cinnaminson, NJ
(609) 786-6885

# Columbus

Columbus Farmers Market & Flea
   Market
Rt. 206 S.
Columbus, NJ
(609) 267-0400
(Call for dates & times)

Living History Shop
18 Tower Dr.
Columbus, NJ
(609) 261-2649

Georgetown Station
35 Chesterfield Rd.
Columbus, NJ
(609) 298-0089

# Crosswicks

Jack & Mary's Antiques
Main St. (Rt. 38)
Crosswicks, NJ
(609) 298-2035

# Edgewater Park

Granny's Treasures
1713 Bridgeboro Rd.
Edgewater Park, NJ
(609) 835-4629

**Fort Dix**

David B. Edwards
P.O. Box 8
Fort Dix, NJ
(609) 231-8362
(Books only, by appt.)

**Hainesport**

Country Antique Center
Rt. 38
Hainesport, NJ
(609) 261-1924/800-264-4694
(Over 90 dealers.)

Ebenezer's Antiques
1325 Rt. 38
Hainesport, NJ
(609) 702-9447

Fox Hill Antiques
2123 Rt. 38
(3 miles East of I-295)
Hainesport, NJ
(609) 518-0200

Rupp's Antiques
2108 Rt. 38
Hainesport, NJ
(609) 267-4848

The Browse Around Shop
2108 Rt. 38
Hainesport, NJ
(609) 261-0274

## Mansfield

Durkins Furniture
448 Valley Rd.
Mansfield Township, NJ
(800) 592-5565

## Maple Shade

Cherry Hill Liquidators, Inc.
105 W. Main St.
Maple Shade, NJ
(609) 321-0742

## Medford

Alley Kat Antiques
6 N. Main St.
Medford Twp., NJ
(609) 714-0441

Spirit of '76
49 N. Main St.
Medford, NJ
(609) 654-2850

Arbor Gate Antiques
16 S. Main St.
Medford, NJ
(609) 654-1200

The Way We Were
4 N. Main St.
Medford, NJ
(609) 654-0343

Mill House Antiques
Church Rd. & Lenape Tr.
Medford, NJ
(609) 953-1402

Toll House Antiques
160 Old Marlton Pike & Hartford Rd.
Medford, NJ
(609) 953-0005

MedfordVillage Antiques Gallery
32 N. Main St.
Medford, NJ
(609) 654-7577

The Swan
1 N. Main St.
Medford, NJ
(609) 654-5252

Recollections
6 N. Main St.
Medford, NJ
(609) 654-1515

Yesterday & Today Shop
Lakes Shopping Center
Medford, NJ
(609) 654-7786

Regina's of Medford Village
6 S. Main St.
Medford, NJ
(609) 654-2521

## Moorestown

Amazing Antiques
300 W. 2nd St.
Moorestown, NJ
(609) 235-4983

Country Peddler Antiques
111 Chester Ave.
Moorestown, NJ
(609) 235-0680

E-B Coins & Stamps
57 E. Main St.
Moorestown, NJ
(609) 235-2463

George Wurtzel Antiques
69 E. Main St.
Moorestown, NJ
(609) 234-9631

Her Own Place
113 E. Main St.
Moorestown,NJ
(609) 234-2445

Kingsway Antiques
527 E. Main St.
Moorestown, NJ
(609) 234-7373
(By appointment.)

Monique's Antiques
Moorestown Mall
Rt. 38 & Lenola Rd.
Moorestown, NJ
(609) 235-7407

Welsh Antiques
301 W. Main St.
Moorestown, NJ
(609) 235-4988

## Mount Holly

Bill's Bargains
15 King St.
Mt. Holly, NJ
(609 261-0096

Center Stage Antiques
41 King St.
Mt. Holly, NJ
(609) 261-0602

Old Glory Antiques
In The Mill Race Shops
Fountain Square
Mt. Holly, NJ
(609) 261-4144

## Mount Laurel

Creek Road Antique Centre Inc.
123 Creek Rd.
Village of Rancocas Woods
Mount Laurel, NJ
(609) 778-8899
(30 dealers)

Collector's Express
104 Berkshire Dr.
Mount Laurel, NJ
(609) 866-1693

## Pemberton

Encore Antiques & Collectibles
108 Hanover St.
Pemberton, NJ
(609) 726-0061

The Alphabet Owl
12 Pemberton-Juliustown Rd.
Pemberton Township, NJ
(609) 894-2335

Grist Mill Antique Center
127 Hanover St. (Rt. 616)
Pemberton, NJ
(609) 726-1588

## Rancocas

Carpet Baggers Emprrium
Creek & Marnehay Rd.
Rancocas Woods, NJ
(609) 234-5095

Spencer's Indoor Antique Market
Spencer Village & 116 Creek Rd.
Rancocas Woods, NJ
(609) 778-2065/222-9555

## Riverside

Irish Dan Used Furniture
12 Scott St.
Riverside, NJ
(609) 764-7042

Pete's Used Furniture & Antiques
119 S. Chester Ave.
Riverside, NJ
(609) 764-9441
(By Appointment.)

## Riverton

Furniture Resale Outlet
523 Howard St.
Riverton, NJ
(609) 829-3300

## Vincentown

Allen's Auction Service
231 Landing St.
Vincentown, NJ
(609) 267-8382

Antique Phonograph & Record Center
Rt. 206
Vincentown, NJ
(609) 859-8617

# Camden County

Barrington
Berlin
Cherry Hill
Collingswood
Gibbsboro
Haddon Heights
Haddonfield
Merchantville
Pennsauken
Runnemeade
Voorhees
Westmont

# Barrington

Potpourri Corner
131 Clements Bridge Rd.
Barrington, NJ
(609) 547-3611

# Berlin

Antiques Plain & Fancy
180 Haddon Ave.
West Berlin, NJ
(609) 767-4805

Winters' Gun Specialties
66 W. White Horse Pike
Berlin, NJ
(609) 767-0349

Wilma Saxton, Inc.
37 Clementon Rd.
Berlin, NJ
(800) 267-8029

# Cherry Hill

Caney Booksellers
One Cherry Hill Mall Dr., Suite 220
Cherry Hill, NJ
(609) 667-7223
(Books only, by appointment)

The White House Antiques
45 Kresson Rd.
Cherry Hill, NJ
(609) 795-6133

Keith's Antiques
Cherry Hill Mall
Cherry Hill, NJ
(609) 488-1066
(Antiques & Reproductions)

# Collingswood

Ashwell's Yesterday's Treasures
738 Haddon Ave.
Collingswood, NJ
(609) 858-6659

The Yesteryear Shop
788 Haddon Ave.
Collingswood, NJ
(609) 854-1786

Collingswood Antiques
812 Haddon Ave.
Collingswood, NJ
(609) 858-9700

Unforgettables
980 Haddon Ave.
Collingswood, NJ
(609) 858-4501

Ellis Antiques
817 Haddon Ave.
Collingswood, NJ
(609) 854-6346

# Gibbsboro

Gibbsboro Book Barn & Bindery
10 Washington Ave.
Gibbsboro, NJ
(609) 435-2525
(Books only)

# Haddon Heights

Haddon Heights Antiques Center
Clements Bridge Rd. & E. Atlantic Ave.
Haddon Heights, NJ
(609) 546-0555
(80 dealers)

# Haddonfield

Adam's Antiques
19 E. Kings Hwy.
Haddonfield, NJ
(609) 854-4696

Cronin & Murphy
13 S. Haddon Ave.
Haddonfield, NJ
(609) 428-8833

Elaine Woodford, Bookseller
Box 68
Haddonfield, NJ
(609) 354-9158
(Books, by appointment.)

Haddonfield Gallery
1 Kings Court
Haddonfield, NJ
(609) 429-7722

Owl's Tale
140 Kings Highway East
E. Haddonfield, NJ
(609) 795-8110

The General Store
37 Ellis St.
Haddonfield, NJ
(609) 428-3707

The Haddonfield Antique Center
9 Kings Hwy.
Haddonfield, NJ
(609) 429-1929

Two in the Attic Antiques &
   Collectibles
3 Kings Court
Haddonfield, NJ
(609) 429-4035

# Merchantville

Between The Covers-Rare Books
35 Maple Ave.
Merchantville, NJ
(609) 665-2284
(Books only)

Green Marquee Antiques
2 E. Maple Ave.
Merchantville, NJ
(609) 910-0055

Hudson's Fine Things
26 S. Center St.
Merchantville, NJ
(609) 317-9227

# Pennsauken

Memories Past
7725 Maple Ave. & Haddonfield Rd.
Pennsauken, NJ
(609) 317-0662

Slots by Bob Levy
2802 Centre St.
Pennsauken, NJ
(609) 663-2554

## Runnemeade

Mary Ann's Antiques
15 N. Black Horse Pike
Runnemeade, NJ
(609) 939-0230

Memorable Investments
115 N. Black Horse Pike
Runnemeade, NJ
(609) 939-3999

Antique & Coin Buyers
Black Horse Pike
Runnemeade, NJ
(609) 931-3131

Seashore Antiques
11 N. Black Horse Pike
Runnemeade, NJ
(609) 939-3939

## Voorhees

Never Again Antiques
99 Rt. 73 & Lake Villa Dr.
Vorhees, NJ
(609) 767-1506
(32 dealers)

Private Estate Liquidators, Inc.
308 Haddonfield Berlin Rd.
Voorhees, NJ
(609) 428-5555

Her Own Place Marcy Lotman
99 State Hwy. 73
Voorhees Twp., NJ
(609) 753-2877

## Westmont

West Jersey Hospital B-Thrifty Shop
225 Haddon Ave.
Westmont, NJ
(609) 854-1003

# Cape May County

Beesley's Point
Cape May
Cape May Courthouse
Cold Spring
Dias Creek
Edgewood
Marmora
North Wildwood
Ocean City
Oceanville
Palermo
Rio Grande
Seaville
South Seaville
Stone Harbor
Swainton
Tuchahoe
Villas
West Cape May
Wildwood

# Beesley's Point

Beesley's Point Antiques
715 N. Shore Rd. (Rt. 9)
Beesley's Point, NJ
(609) 390-3732/390-1691

# Cape May

Acquisitions
Congress Hall
251 Beach Dr.
Cape May, NJ
(609) 884-0006

Aleathea's Antique Shop
Inn of Cape May Lobby
Ocean St. & Beach Dr.
Cape May, NJ
(609) 884-3500

Antique Doorknob
600 Park Blvd.
Cape May, NJ
(609) 884-6282

Cape Island Antiques
609 Jefferson St.
Cape May, NJ
(609) 884-6028

Hazard Sealander Antiques Interiors
479-West Perry St.
Cape May, NJ
(609) 884-0040

K's Used Furniture & Flea Market
Bayview Rd. & Rt. 9
Cape May, NJ
(609) 465-9767

Kate's Antiques & Collectibles
513 Carpenter's Lane
Cape May, NJ
(609) 884-3401

Laurels
24 Decatur St.
Cape May, NJ
(609) 898-1004

Mid Summer Night's Dream
668 Washington St.
Cape May, NJ
(609) 884-1380

Millstone Antiques & Collectibles
742 Seashore Rd. at Cox Lane
Cape May, NJ
(609) 884-5155

Nostalgia Shop
408 Washington St.
Cape May, NJ
(609) 884-7071

Seahorse Antique Center
1129 Rt. 109
Cape May, NJ
(609) 884-8866

Stephanie's Antiques
318 Washington St.
Cape May, NJ
(609) 884-0289

Tabby House Antiques &
  Comfortables
479 W. Perry St.
Cape May, NJ
(609) 898-0908

The Garden Gate
670 Washington Square
Cape May, NJ
(609) 898-1616

Travis Cove
621 Lafayette St.
Cape May, NJ
(609) 884-5959/678-2302

Triple Five Shop
555 Elmire
Cape May, NJ
(609) 884-5864

Victorious Antiques
Congress Hall
251 Beach Dr.
Cape May, NJ
(609) 898-1777/884-1777

# Cape May Courthouse

David Crafts Antiques
589 Stone Harbor Blvd.
Cape May Courthouse, NJ
(609) 465-6082

The Carousel
1563 Rt. 9 North (Swainton)
Cape May Courthouse, NJ
(609) 465-7135

Delsea Cottage Antiques
116 Rt. 47 (Dias Creek)
Cape May Courthouse, NJ
(609) 465-9420

The Gingerbread House
Rt. 9 North (Swainton)
Cape May Courthouse, NJ
(609) 465-9234

Golden Pond Antiques
2089 Rt. 9 North (Clermont)
Cape May Courthouse, NJ
(609) 624-0608

Victorian Cottage Antiques
20 N. Main St.
Cape May Courthouse, NJ
(609) 465-2132

# Cold Spring

House of Old
731 Townbank Rd.
Cold Spring, NJ
(609) 884-1458

Millstone Antique Mall
742 Seashore Rd.
Cold Springs, NJ
(609) 884-5155

# Dias Creek

Ken's Antiques & Furniture
   Restoration
22 Rt. 47 N.
Dias Creek, NJ
(609) 463-8987

# Edgewood

K's Indoor Flea Market
Rt. 9 & Bayview Rd.
Edgewood, NJ
(609) 465-9767

# Marmora

Fred Peech Antiques
1008 S. Shore Rd.
Marmora, NJ
(609) 390-1873

# North Wildwood

Miracle Antiques & Gifts
501 W. Spruce Ave.
North Wildwood, NJ
(609) 523-0031

# Ocean City

Avant Garden
742 Haven Ave.
Ocean City, NJ
(609) 399-7860

Back In Time Antiques, Used
   Furniture & Consignment
1337 West Ave.
Ocean City, NJ
(609) 399-2234

B's Fantasy
11th & Boardwalk
Ocean City, NJ
(609) 398-9302/823-5622

Kay Jay's Doll Emporium
18 East 9th St.
Ocean City, NJ
(609) 399-5632
Joseph's Antiques
908 Asbury Ave.
Ocean City, NJ
(609) 398-3855/398-2984

Only Yesterday
1108 Boardwalk
Ocean City, NJ
(609) 398-2869

Toyrareum
1101 Asbury Ave.
Ocean City, NJ
(609) 391-0480

Yesterday's Best
2748 Asbury Ave.
Ocean City, NJ
(609) 391-9042

Yours, Mine and Ours
33rd and West Ave.
Ocean City, NJ
(609) 525-0270

Buying 1 Piece
To Entire Contents

Free Furniture
Removal

*Back In Time*
Used Furniture - Antiques
And Collectables
1337 West Ave. O. C. NJ

Auctioneer Services
Professional House
Cleanouts

Phone 609-399-2234
JEFF or VAL

## Oceanville

Seafarer Antiques
Rt. 9 & Lilly Lake Rd.
Oceanville, NJ
(609) 652-9491

## Palermo

Rail Road Crossing Antiques
1143 Shore Rd.
Palermo, NJ
(609) 390-1833

## Rio Grande

Rodia Used Furniture
2500 Rt. 9 South
Rio Grande, NJ
(609) 465-5865

## Seaville

Grandma's Attic Co-Op
3071 Rt. 9
Seaville, NJ
(609) 624-1989

The Antiquarian
3050 Rt. 9
Seaville, NJ
(609) 624-0878

## South Seaville

The Roadrunner Antique Mall
300 Main St.
South Seaville/Dennis Township, NJ
(609) 624-9730/624-0393

## Stone Harbor

Stephen Christopher's Antiques & Collectibles
255 96th St.
Stone Harbor, NJ
(609) 368-0575

The
# *August Farmhouse*
antiques & decorative accessories

Porcelain
Art Glass
Sterling Silver

*"The Jersey Cape's must-see antique shop."*

Lamps, Mirrors
Furniture & More
Estate Appraisals

Route 9, Swainton, NJ  609-465-5135  *All major credit cards accepted.*

## Swainton

Oak Tree Antiques
1401 Rt. 9 N.
Swainton, NJ
(609) 465-1592

The August Farmhouse Antiques
1759 Rt. 9 N.
Swainton, NJ
(609) 465-5135/465-5235

Mallard Lake Antiques
1781 Rt. 9 North (Clermont)
Swainton, NJ
(609) 465-7189
(china & glass)

The Dutch Rose
1842 Rt. 9
Swainton, NJ
(609) 463-0844

# Tuckahoe

The Four Y's
2371 Mosquito Landing Rd. (Rt.50)
Tuckahoe, NJ
(609) 628-2721

Yesteryear
2235 Rt. 50
Tuckahoe, NJ
(609) 628-2478

Tuckahoe Station Antiques
2261 Rt. 50
Tuckahoe, NJ
(609) 628-2372

Yesteryear Two
2245 Rt. 50
Tuckahoe, NJ
(609) 628-2384

# Villas

St. Anthony's Estate Tag Sale
901 Bayshore Rd.
Villas, NJ
(609) 889-2599

# West Cape May

Bridgetowne Antiques
523 Broadway
West Cape May, NJ
(609) 884-8107

Promises Collectibles
301 N. Broadway
West Cape May, NJ
(609) 884-4411

Jim Bogwater Antiques
201 N. Broadway
West Cape May, NJ
(609) 884-5558

Rocking Horse Antique Center
405 W. Perry St.
West Cape May, NJ
(609) 898-0737

# Wildwoood

Cornerstone/Eagles Nest Thrift Shop
4516 Pacific Ave.
Wildwood, NJ
(609) 523-0875

# Cumberland County

**Bridgeton**
**Deerfield**
**Fairton**
**Heislerville**
**Mauricetown**
**Millville**
**Shiloh**
**Vineland**

# Bridgeton

Cole Bros. Antiques Collectibles &
  Auctioneering
Fairton Rd.
Bridgeton, NJ
(609) 451-1340

The Squirrel's Nest
680 Shiloh Pike (Rt. 49)
Bridgeton, NJ
(609) 455-6594/451-1206

Tracy's Corner
62 N. Laurel St.
Bridgeton, NJ
(609) 455-2160

---

Antiques and Collectibles

# The Squirrel's Nest

HOURS THURSDAY THRU SATURDAY
11A.M. TO 4 P.M.

(609) 455-6594
(609) 451-1206

680 SHILOH PIKE
BRIDGETON, NJ 08302

---

# Deerfield

Deerfield Village
1530 Rt. 77
Deerfield, NJ
(609) 451-2143
(18 dealers)

# Fairton

Carriage House Signs 'n Things
Bridgeton-Fairton Rd.
Fairton, NJ
(609) 455-6400

# Heislerville

Wood Pump Antiques
206 Main St.
Heislerville, NJ
(609) 785-0237

## Mauricetown

Boxwood & Ivy Antiques
9087 Highland St.
Mauricetown, NJ
(609) 785-1246

Mary's Antiques
9070 Highland St.
Mauricetown, NJ
(609) 785-2686

Maurice River Antiques & Gifts
1207 Front St.
Mauricetown, NJ
(609) 785-9428

The Cook House Antiques
9530 Highland St.
Mauricetown, NJ
(609) 785-1137

Tulip Tree Antiques
South St.
Mauricetown, NJ
(609) 785-0850

Wagon Wheel
9086 Highland St.
Mauricetown, NJ
(609) 785-0278

## Millville

Wind Chimes Book Exchange
210 High St.
Millville, NJ
(609) 327-3714
(Books only)

## Shiloh

Shiloh Antique Shoppe
Rt. 49 at blinker light
Shiloh, NJ
(609) 453-1800

## Vineland

Rose Petal Treasures
1199 S. Main Rd.
Vineland, NJ
(609) 794-8300

U Sell Flea Market
Vineland Area
(609) 691-1222
(Call for hours & Directions)

# Essex County

Belleville
Caldwell
Cedar Grove
East Orange
Fairfield
Irvington
Maplewood
Millburn
Montclair
Newark
Roseland
Short Hills
South Orange
Verona
West Caldwell
West Orange

## Belleville

Brookside Books
49 Ralph St.
Belleville, NJ
(973) 744-0685

Second Hand Rose
203 Washington Ave.
Belleville, NJ
(973) 759-0019

## Caldwell

Anne Filkin Lamps & Shades
328 Bloomfield Ave.
Caldwell, NJ
(973) 228-9038

Book Heaven
Box 371
Caldwell, NJ
(973) 228-5927
(Books only, by appointment.)

## Cedar Grove

The Mulberry Bush
496 Pompton Ave.
Cedar Grove, NJ
(973) 239-9357

## East Orange

Antiques Etc.
194 Central Ave.
East Orange, NJ
(973) 678-0011

## Fairfield

Masterpiece Home Furniture
257 Rt. 46
Fairfield, NJ
(973) 808-9080

## Irvington

Alice's Antiques
1264 Springfield Ave.
Irvington, NJ
(973) 372-6612

Antiques, Lace & Things
125 Springfield Ave.
Irvington, NJ
(973) 416-2177

## Maplewood

Bee & Thistle Antiques
89 Baker St.
Maplewood, NJ
(973) 763-3166

Renaissance Antiques
410 Ridgewood Rd.
Maplewood, NJ
(973) 761-7654/761-7450

Erik Mathias Designs
201 Parker Ave.
Maplewood, NJ
(973) 378-2040

The Grey Swan
411 Ridgewood Rd.
Maplewood, NJ
(973) 763-0660

On Track Antiques
Maplewood Ave. & Depot Place
Maplewood, NJ
(973) 763-4514
(By appointment)

# Millburn

Forgotten Times
27 Main St.
Millburn, NJ
(201) 376-4148

## Montclair

American Sampler Inc.
26 Church St.
Montclair, NJ
(973) 744-1474

Antique Liquidators
662 Bloomfield Ave.
Montclair, NJ
(973) 746-8948

Antique Star
627 Bloomfield Ave.
Montclair, NJ
(973) 746-0070

Beam Me Up, Watson!
358½ Lamington Rd.
Montclair, NJ
(973) 744-7373
(Books only)

Bill Sablon Antiques
411 Bloomfield Ave.
Montclair, NJ
(973) 726-4397

Browser's Nook
322 Orange Rd.
Montclair, NJ
(973) 744-1619

Century Antiques
223 Glenridge Ave.
Montclair, NJ
(973) 783- 7174

Chameleon Antiques
97 Walnut St.
Montclair, NJ
(973) 655-9190

Class Act Antiques & Collectibles
415 Bloomfield Ave.
Montclair, NJ
(973) 746-9543

Earl Roberts Antiques & Interiors
17 S. Fullerton Ave.
Montclair, NJ
(973) 744-2232

Edward's Antiques
55 N. Fullerton Ave.
Montclair Area, NJ
(973) 783-9352

Gallery of Vintage
504 Bloomfield Ave.
Montclair, NJ
(973) 509-1201

Garage Sale
194 Claremont Ave.
Montclair, NJ
(973) 783-0806

Georgiana Stockel
80 S. Mountain Ave.
Montclair, NJ
(973) 744-5642

Jackie's Antiques
51 North Fullerton Ave.
Montclair, NJ
(973) 744-7972

Maps of Antiquity
Montclair Area
(973) 744-4364
(Antique Maps by appointment only.)

Martin William Antiques & Home
   Decor
41 Church St.
Montclair, NJ
(973) 744-1149

Mary Wood Estate & Home Sales
94 Yantacaw Brook Road
Upper Montclair, NJ
(973) 783-2942/783-9352

Milt's Antiques
662 Bloomfield Ave.
Montclair, NJ
(973) 746-4445

Montclair Book Center
221 Glenridge Ave.
Montclair, NJ
(973) 783-3630
(Books only)

Morgan Elliot Antiques
244 Bellevue Ave.
Upper Montclair, NJ
(973) 746-2266

Noel's Place
173 Glenridge Ave.
Montclair, NJ
(973) 744-2156

Past & Present Resale Shop
416 Bloomfield Ave.
Montclair, NJ
(973) 746-8871

Patterson Smith
23 Prospect Terrace
Montclair, NJ
(973) 744-3291
(Books, by appointment.)

Persia Oriental Rugs, Inc.
500 Bloomfield Ave.
Montclair, NJ
(973) 744-3731

Station West Antiques
225 Glenridge Ave.
Montclair, NJ
(973) 744-9370

The Ivory Bird Antiques
555 Bloomfield Ave.
Montclair, NJ
(973) 744-5225

The Way We Were Antiques
15 Midland Ave.
Montclair, NJ
(973) 783-1111

Threadneedle Street
195 Bellevue Ave.
Upper Montclair, NJ
(973) 783-1336

Trent Antiques
436 Bloomfield Ave.
Montclair, NJ
(973) 783-4676

Yesterday's Books & Records
559 Bloomfield Ave.
Montclair, NJ
(973) 744-7223
(Books & records)

## Newark

AJS Antique Restorations
84 Lockwood St.
Newark, NJ
(973) 491-9277

## Roseland

Tina's Ephemeral Editions
54 Pitcairn Dr.
Roseland, NJ
(973) 228-5453
(Books, by appointment.)

## Short Hills

J & J Hanrahan ABAA
320 White Oak Ridge Rd.
Short Hills, NJ
(973) 912-8907
(Books only, by appointment.)

## South Orange

Aaltglen's Galleries
461 Irvington Ave.
South Orange, NJ
(973) 762-7200

Carrie Topf Antiques
50 W. South Orange Ave.
South Orange, NJ
(973) 762-8773

Alan Angele Popular Culture
350 Turrell Ave.
South Orange, NJ
(973) 378-5822
(Books only)

## Verona

June Emrich Antiques
282 Bloomfield Ave.
Verona, NJ
(973) 857-9144

## West Caldwell

Gibson Galleries
14 Kramer Ave.
West Caldwell, NJ
(973) 403-9377
(Books only, by appointment.)

## West Orange

Cherished Memories
475 Valley Rd.
West Orange, NJ
(973) 672-4646

In Days of Old Antiques
173 Main St.
West Orange, NJ
(973) 325-7955

# Gloucester County

Bridgeport

Clarksboro

Greenwich

Malaga

Mickletown

Mullica Hill

Newfield

Pitman

Repaupo

Turnersville

West Deptford

Woodbury

## Bridgeport

Raccoon Creek Antiques
20 Main St.
Bridgeport, NJ
(609) 467-3197

## Clarksboro

Boggs Boynton Antiques
186 Timberlane Rd.
Clarksboro, NJ
(609) 224-1165

Karl Dreibach & Company
186 Timberlane Rd.
Clarksboro, NJ
(609) 224-0266

## Greenwich

East Greenwich Industrial Park
Timberlane Rd.
E. Greenwich Township, NJ
(609) 423-3227
(6 dealers)

The Ye Griffin
YeGreate St.
Greenwich, NJ
(609) 451-5867

## Malaga

Mike's Used Furniture & Antiques
559 Rt. 47S
Malaga, NJ
(609) 694-3005/694-0635

Scotland Run Antiques
3485 Rt. 40
Malaga, NJ
(609) 694-3344

Verne C. Streeter
Rt. 40 & Malaga Park Dr.
Malaga, NJ
(609) 694-4163

## Mickletown

Dutch Auction Sales
356 Swedesboro Ave.
Mickletown, NJ
(609) 423-7857
(Call for auction dates & times.)

## Mullica Hill

Antiquities at Mullica Hill
43 S. Main St.
Mullica Hill, NJ
(609) 478-6773

Carriage House Antiques
62 N. Main St.
Mullica Hill, NJ
(609) 478-4459

Debra's Dolls
20 N. Main St. (The Mullica House)
Mullica Hill, NJ
(609) 478-9778

Deja Vu Antique & Gift Gallery
38 S. Main St.
Mullica Hill, NJ
(609) 478-6351

Elizabeth's of Mullica Hill
32 N. Main St.
Mullica Hill, NJ
(609) 478-6510

June Bug Antiques
44 S. Main St.
Mullica Hill, NJ
(609) 478-2167/646-7841

King's Row Antique Center
46 N. Main St.
Mullica Hill, NJ
(609) 478-4361

Lynne Antiques
49 S. Main St.
Mullica Hill, NJ
(609) 223-9199/PA (610) 626-7187

Mame's on Main Street
13 S. Main St.
Mullica Hill, NJ
(609) 223-0555

Murphy's Loft
53 N. Main St. (Rt 322)
Mullica Hill, NJ
(609) 478-4928
(books, prints, paper, maps &
  magazines)

Raccoon's Tale
6 High St.
Mullica Hill, NJ
(609) 478-4488

Sugar & Spice Antiques
45 Main St.
Mullica Hill, NJ
(609) 478-2622

The Antique Corner At Mullica Hill
45 N. Main St.
Mullica Hill, NJ
(609) 478-4754

The Antique Warehouse
2 S. Main St.
Mullica Hill, NJ
(609) 478-4500

The Clock Shop
45 S. Main St.
Mullica Hill, NJ
(609) 478-6555

The Front Porch Antiques
21S Main St.
Mullica Hill, NJ
(609) 478-6556

The Old Gray Mare
54 S. Main St.
Mullica Hill, NJ
(609) 478-6229

The Old Mill Antique Mall
1 S. Main St. (Rt. 45)
Mullica Hill, NJ
(609) 478-9810

The Old Post Shoppes
50 S. Main St.
Mullica Hill, NJ
(609) 478-2910

The Queen's Inn Antiques
48 N. Main St.
Mullica Hill, NJ
(609) 456-7545

The Royal Crescent
37 S. Main St.
Mullica Hill, NJ
(609) 223-0220

The Sign of St. George Antiques
30 S. Main St.
Mullica Hill, NJ
(609) 478-6101

## Mullica Hill (continued)

The Treasure Chest
50 S. Main St.
Mullica Hill, NJ
(609) 468-4371

The Yellow Garage Antiques
66 S. Main St.
Mullica Hill, NJ
(609) 478-0300

## Newfield

Raven's Antiques
1888 (Rt. 40)
Newfield, NJ
(609) 697-3622

The Old Barn
226 N. West Blvd.
Newfield, NJ
(609) 697-3242

## Pitman

Another Man's Treasure
16 S. Broadway Ave.
Pitman, NJ
(609) 589-7299

Foley's Idle Hour
162 S. Broadway Ave.
Pitman, NJ
(609) 582-0510
(Books only)

## Repaupo

James Transue Antiques
The Annex Galleries
Repaupo Station Rd.
Repaupo, NJ
(609) 467-4080

S & S Auctions
Repaupo Station Rd.
Repaupo, NJ
(609) 467-3778
(Auctions every other Tuesday,
    8:00 am.)

## Richwood

Clems Run Antiques
307 Richwood Rd.
Richwood, NJ
(609) 863-1625

## Turnersville

Antique Trains
Greentree Rd & Lantern Lane
Turnersville, NJ
(609) 589-6224

## West Deptford

Amaridios Antiques, Inc.
1501 Grandview Ave.
West Deptford, NJ
(609) 848-4447

## Woodbury

Buy Gones Auction
Broad & Centre Sts.
Woodbury, NJ
(609) 251-9505
(Auctions held every other Sunday)

Posh Pomegranate Antiques Mall
66 S. Broad St. (Rt.45)
Woodbury, NJ
(609) 853-1544

# Hudson County

**Bayonne**
**Bergen**
**Guttenburg**
**Hoboken**
**Jersey City**
**New Hampton**
**North Bergen**
**West New York**

## Bayonne

Affordable Antique Buyers
625 John F. Kennedy Blvd.
Bayonne, NJ
(201) 339-2800

Antiques by Angela & Deborah
922 Broadway (44th St.)
Bayonne, NJ
(201) 823-1148

Bargain Hunter's Den
444 Avenue C
Bayonne, NJ
(201) 339-7026

Castle Clock Shop
745 Broadway
Bayonne, NJ
(201) 823-1160

## Bergen

Now & Then
140 Allendale Ave.
Bergen, NJ
(201) 934-1440

## Guttenburg

Vintage Castings Inc.
6709 Park Avenue
Guttenburg, NJ
(201) 861-2979

## Hoboken

Erie Street Antiques
533 Washington St.
Hoboken, NJ
(201) 656-3596/(973) 378-9036

Fat Cat Antiques
57 Newark St.
Hoboken, NJ
(201) 222-5454

Ferenc Antiques & Collectibles
703 Garden St.
Hoboken, NJ
(201) 798-2441

Hoboken Antiques
511 Washington St.
Hoboken, NJ
(201) 659-7329

House Ware Inc.
628 Washington St.
Hoboken, NJ
(201) 659-6009

Little Cricket Antiques
12th St.
Hoboken, NJ
(201) 222-6270

Michelle Antiques/"The Old Time
  House"
402 Grand St.
Hoboken, NJ
(201) 222-6167

The Mission Position
1122 Washington St.
Hoboken, NJ
(201) 656-3398

United Decorating Co. Inc.
421 Washington St.
Hoboken, NJ
(201) 659-1922

## Jersey City

Cliff's Clocks
400 7th St.
Jersey City, NJ
(201) 798-7510

Portfolio Inc.
498 Jersey Ave.
Jersey City, NJ
(201) 332-1311

L & L Antiques
1170 Summit Ave.
Jersey City, NJ
(201) 656-6928

Retro Antiques
3514 John F. Kennedy Blvd.
Jersey City, NJ
(201) 656-6139

## New Hampton

The Attic Antiques
210 Muconetong Rd.
New Hampton, NJ
(908) 537-6662

## North Bergen

Park Antiques
9001 River Rd.
North Bergen, NJ
(201) 943-7828

## West New York

The Tickled Pink Petunia
6703 Park Ave.
West New York, NJ
(201) 869-5829

The Tickled Pink Petunia II
6718 Park Ave.
West New York, NJ
(201) 869-5829

# Hunterdon County

Annandale
Califon
Clinton
Flemington
Frenchtown
Glen Gardner
Lambertville
Lebanon
Milford
Mountainville
Oldwick
Pittstown
Pottersville
Rosemont
Whitehouse Station

## Annandale

Everything Country
1451 Rt. 22
Annandale, NJ
(908) 236-2495

Golden Rainbow
96 Beaver Ave.
Annandale, NJ
(908) 730-6603

## Califon

44 Main Street Antiques
44 Main St.
Califon, NJ
(908) 832-2910

James B. Grievo Antiques
60 Sawmill Rd.
Califon, NJ
(908) 439-2147

## Clinton

Art's Resale
1751 Rt. 31 N.
Clinton, NJ
(908) 735-4442

Paddy-Wak Antiques
19 1/2 Old Highway 22
Clinton, NJ
(908) 735-9770

McCoy's Rare Books
21 Austin Hill Rd.
Clinton, NJ
(908) 713-6720
(Books only, by appointment.)

Rockinghorse Antiques
Rt. 57 Port Murray Lane
Clinton, NJ
(908) 689-2813

Memories
21 Main St.
Clinton, NJ
(908) 730-9096

Weathervane Antiques
18A Main St.
Clinton, NJ
(908) 730-0877

## Flemington

55 Main Antiques
55 Main St.
Flemington, NJ
(908) 788-2605

Country Pine Antiques
14 Fulper Rd.
Flemington, NJ
(908) 806-0203

Antiques Emporium
32 Church St.
Flemington, NJ
(908) 782-5077
(60 dealers)

Den of Antiquity
150 Main St.
Flemington, NJ
(908) 806-3888

B & M Flemington Antique Center
24 Main St.
Flemington, NJ
(908) 806-8841

Furstover Antiques
505 Stanton Station Rd.
Flemington, NJ
(908) 782-3513

Consignment Collections
9 Central Ave.
Flemington, NJ
(908) 788-0103

Liberty Antiques
35 Fulper Rd.
Flemington, NJ
(908) 782-5524
(Multi-dealer shop.)

# Flemington (continued)

Main Street Antique Center
156 Main St.
Flemington, NJ
(908) 788-6767

Popkorn Antiques
4 Mine St.
Flemington, NJ
(908) 782-9631

Quiet Rainbow
17 Church St.
Flemington, NJ
(908) 284-1255

Sandlot Sports Cards & Collectables
16 Main St.
Flemington, NJ
(908) 284-9242

The Hunterdon Exchange
155 Main St.
Flemington, NJ
(908) 782-6229

The Little House of Treasures
755 Rt. 202
Flemington, NJ
(908) 806-6262

The People's Bookshop
160 Main St.
Flemington, NJ
(908) 369-4488
(By chance)

## Frenchtown

Brook's Antiques
24 Bridge St.
Frenchtown, NJ
(908) 996-7161

Jeanine-Louise Antiques
8 Race St.
Frenchtown, NJ
(908) 996-3520

JM Home
29 Bridge St.
Frenchtown, NJ
(908) 996-0442

Running Fox Antiques
49 Bridge St.
Frenchtown, NJ
(908) 996-7391

The Mews
29 Race St.
Frenchtown, NJ
(908) 996-0433

Variete
43 Bridge St.
Frenchtown, NJ
(908) 996-7876

## Glen Gardner

Hunt House Antiques
Rt. 31
Glen Gardner, NJ
(908) 537-7044

## Lambertville

America Antiques
S. Main St.
Lambertville, NJ
(609) 397-6966

Antiques by Rossi
285 S. Main St.
Lambertville, NJ
(609) 397-1599

Archangel Antiques
43 N. Union St.
Lambertville, NJ
(609) 397-4333

Artfull Eye
12 N. Union St.
Lambertville, NJ
(609) 397-8115

Best of France Antiques
204 N. Union St.
Lambertville, NJ
(609) 397-9881

Blue Raccoon
6 Coryelle St.
Lambertville, NJ
(609) 397-1900

Bridge Street Antiques
75 Bridge St.
Lambertville, NJ
(609) 397-9890

Broadmoor Antiques
6 N. Union St.
Lambertville, NJ
(609) 397-8802

Center City Antiques
11 Kline's Court
Lambertville, NJ
(609) 397-9886

Coryell Street Antiques
51 Coryell St.
Lambertville, NJ
(609) 397-5700

David Rago's 333 North Main Street
    Antiques & Auction Center
333 N. Main St.
Lambertville, NJ
(609) 397-7330

E.H. Limited
8 Bridge St.
Lambertville, NJ
(609) 397-4411

Evelyn Gordon
28 N. Union
Lambertville, NJ
(609) 397-3589

Fran Jay Antiques
10 Church St.
Lambertville, NJ
(609) 397-1571

Friarswood Antiques
36 Coryell
Lambertsville, NJ
(609) 397-2133

Garden House Antiques
39 N. Union St.
Lambertville, NJ
(609) 397-9797

Gloria N. Greenwald Antiques & Folk
    Art
45 Clinton St.
Lambertville, NJ
(609) 397-9424

Golden Nugget Antique Flea Market
Rt. 29
Lambertville, NJ
(609) 397-0811

Greenbranch Antiques
3 Lambert Lane
Lambertville, NJ
(609) 397-1225

H. & C. Eick's Antiques
54 N. Union St.
Lambertville, NJ
(609) 397-8485

H & H Home Antiques
37 N. Union St.
Lambertville, NJ
(609) 397-9400

H K H Inc.
14 Church St.
Lambertville, NJ
(609) 397-4141

Helena Castella Antique & Fine
    Furnishings
14 Bridge St.
Lambertville, NJ
(609) 397-7274

Heritage Antique Lighting
67 Bridge St.
Lambertville, NJ
(609) 397-8820

It's A Wonderful Life
63 Bridge St.
Lambertville, NJ
(609) 397-9557

JRJ Home, Ltd.
7 N. Union St.
Lambertville, NJ
(609) 397-3800

Jack's Furniture & Antiques
56 Coryelle St.
Lambertville, NJ
(609) 397-2632

Jim's Antiques Limited
6 Bridge St.
Lambertville, NJ
(609) 397-7700

Joan Evans Antiques
48 Coryelle St.
Lambertville, NJ
(609) 397-7726

Karen & David Dutch Antiques
22 Bridge St.
Lambertville, NJ
(609) 397-2288

Kelly McDowell Fine Art & Antiques
38 Coryelle St.
Lambertville, NJ
(609) 397-4465

King Charles, Ltd. & The Drawing
  Room
32 Bridge St.
Lambertville, NJ
(609) 397-9733

Kyle Kitner's Antiques & Collectibles
28 N. Union St.
Lambertville, NJ
(609) 397-8618

Lambertville Antique Market
1864 River Rd.
Lambertville, NJ
(609) 397-0456

Lambertville's Bridge Street Antiques
15 Bridge St.
Lambertville, NJ
(609) 397-9890

Lambertville's Center City Antiques
11 Kline Court
Lambertville, NJ
(609) 397-9886

Lambertville Gallery of Fine Art
20 N. Union St.
Lambertville, NJ
(609) 397-4121

Left Bank Books
28 N. Union St.
Lambertville, NJ
(609) 397-4966
(Books only)

Lovrinic's Antiques
15 N. Union St.
Lambertville, NJ
(609) 397-8600

Meld
53 N. Union St.
Lambertville, NJ
(609) 397-8487/8600

Mill Crest Antiques
72 Bridge St.
Lambertville, NJ
(609) 259-0659/397-4700

Miller-Topia Designers
35 N. Union
Lambertville, NJ
(609) 397-9339

Morningstar Carriage House
  Antiques, Arts & Collectibles
7 N. Main St.
Lambertville, NJ
(609) 397-0877

Olde English Pine
202 N. Union St.
(Corner of Elm & N. Union)
Lambertville, NJ
(609) 397-4978

Optique Gallery/ The Gallery
28 N. Union
Lambertville, NJ
(609) 397-2121

Park Place Antique Jewelry
6 Bridge St.
Lambertville, NJ
(609) 397-0102

Perrault -Rago Gallery
17 S. Main St.
Lambertville, NJ
(609) 397-1802

Passiflora
54 Coryell
Lambertville, NJ
(609) 397-1010

Pedersen Gallery
17 N. Union
Lambertville, NJ
(609) 397-1332

Peter Wallace Antiques
5 Lambert Lane
Lambertville, NJ
(609) 397-4914

Phoenix Books
49 N. Union St.
Lambertville, NJ
(609) 397-4960
(Books)

Porkyard Antiques
8 Coryell St.
Lambertville, NJ
(609) 397-2088

Prestige Antiques
287 S. Main St.
The Laceworks Bldg.
Lambertville,NJ
(609) 397-2400

Redux
16 Church St.
Lambertville, NJ
(609) 397-0303

Robert H. Yaroschuk Antiques
10 N. Union St.
Lambertville, NJ
(609) 397-8886

Robin's Egg Gallery
24 N. Union St.
Lambertville, NJ
(609) 397-9137

Rossi Antiques
285 S. Main St.
Lambertville, NJ
(609) 397-1599

Stefon's Antiques
29 Bridge St.
Lambertville, NJ
(609) 397-8609

Taylor's Country Store
28 N. Union St.
Lambertville, NJ
(609) 397-8816

The 5 & Dime
40 N. Union St.
Lambertville, NJ
(609) 397-4957

The Drawing Room & King Charles
   Ltd.
36 S. Main St.
Lambertville, NJ
(609) 397-7977

The Old Carriage House
51 Bridge St.
Lambertville, NJ
(609) 397-3331

The Orchard Hill Collection
22 N. Union St.
Lambertville, NJ
(609) 397-1188

The People's Store
28 N. Union St.
Lambertville, NJ
(609) 397-9808

# Lambertville (continued)

Undercover Underfoot
12 Church St.
Lambertville, NJ
(609) 397-0044

Weaver Antiques & Fine Furnishings
9-B Church
Lambertville, NJ
(609) 397-4171

## Lebanon

Jantiques
1261 Rt. 31
Lebanon, NJ
(908) 735-4009

Lebanon Antique Center Corp.
1211 Rt. 22
Lebanon, NJ
(908) 236-6616

## Milford

Gary's Antiques
638 Rt. 627
Milford, NJ
(908) 995-2750

## Mountainville

Nancy & Alan Gilbert Antiques
3 Main St.
Mountainville, NJ
(908) 234-1486

## Oldwick

Collections
152 Oldwick Rd. (Rt. 523)
Oldwick, NJ
(908) 439-3736

The Magic Shop
60 Main St.
Oldwick, NJ
(908) 439-2330

Keeping Room Antiques
53 Main St. (Rt. 517)
Oldwick, NJ
(908) 439-3701

The Snow Goose at Oldwick
39 Old Turnpike Rd.
Oldwick, NJ
(908) 439-3344

## Pittstown

Jan's Vintage Textiles
At the Sky Manor Airport
Pittstown, NJ
(908) 996-1000

Provenance Auction Associates
Sky Manor Rd.
Pittstown, NJ
(908) 996-7505
(Call for auction dates & times.)

## Pottersville

Moonlight Mile Antiques
10 Black River Rd.
Pottersville, NJ
(908) 439-3337

The Mill
Fairmount Rd. (East)
Pottersville, NJ
(908) 439-2724/439-3803
(Books & prints)

# Rosemont

Lots of Time Shop
78 Rt. 519
Rosemont, NJ
(609) 397-0890

# Whitehouse Station

Antique Clock Gallery
137 Main St.
Whitehouse Station, NJ
(908) 534-6070
(Clocks & Fine Art)

Old & New
424 Rt. 22
Whitehouse Station, NJ
(908) 534-8646

# Mercer County

Ewing
Hamilton Township
Hightstown
Hopewell
Mercerville
Princeton
Trenton

# Ewing

Estate Galleries Ltd.
1641 N. Olden Ave.
Ewing, NJ
(609) 219-0300

# Hamilton Township

Greenwood Antiques
1918 Greenwood Ave.
Hamilton Twp, NJ
(609) 586-6887
(Art Books & paintings, by
   appointment.)

# Hightstown

A-A Empire Antiques
278 Monmouth St.
Hightstown, NJ
(609) 426-0820/(800) 626-4969

Conover Antiques
780 York Road (Rt. 539)
Hightstown, NJ
(609) 448-0269

Olde Country Antiques
346 Franklin St.
Hightstown, NJ
(609) 448-2670

# Hopewell

Attics Annex
15 Seminary Ave.
Hopewell, NJ
(609) 466-0025

Brian Gage Antiques
33 W. Broad St.
Hopewell, NJ
(609) 466-1722

H. Clark Interiors
31 W. Broad
Hopewell, NJ
(609) 397-3885

Hopewell Antique Center
Hamilton Avenue & Somerset St.
Hopewell, NJ
(609) 466-2990

Hopewell Antique Cottage
8 Somerset St.
Hopewell, NJ
(609) 466-1810

Hope Spring Antiques
35 W. Broad St.
Hopewell, NJ
(609) 466-0556

Ninotchka
35 W. Broad St.
Hopewell, NJ
(609) 466-0556

On Military Matters
31 W. Broad St.
Hopewell, NJ
(609) 466-2329
(Books only)

Pennfield Antiques
47 W. Broad St. (Rt. 518)
Hopewell, NJ
(609) 466-0827

Tomato Factory Antique Center
Hamilton Ave. (At end of street)
Hopewell, NJ
(609) 466-9833

Voulas World II
43 W. Broad St.
Hopewell, NJ
(609) 466-8292

## Mercerville

David Stout
47 Jefferson Ave.
Mercerville, NJ
(609) 586-2149

Richard Conti Antiques
52 Rt. 33
Mercerville, NJ
(609) 584-1080

## Princeton

Bryn Mawr Bookshop
Arts Council
102 Witherspoon St.
Princeton, NJ
(609) 921-7479
(Books only)

Collectors' Editions
P.O. Box 7005
Princeton, NJ
(609) 520-1669
(Books, by appointment.)

East & West Antiques
4451 Rt. 27
Princeton, NJ
(609) 924-2743

Eye For Art
6 Spring St.
Princeton, NJ
(609) 924-5277

Gilded Lion
4 Chambers St.
Princeton, NJ
(609) 924-6350

Joseph J. Felcone, Inc.
P.O. Box 366
Princeton, NJ
(609) 924-0539
(Books, by appointment.)

Skilman Furniture Store
212 Alexander St.
Princeton, NJ
(609) 924-1881

Tamara's Things
4206 Quaker Bridge Rd.
Princeton, NJ
(609) 452-1567

The Silver Shop
59 Palmer Square W.
Princeton, NJ
(609) 924-2026

Witherspoon Art & Book Store
12 Nassua St.
Princeton, NJ
(609) 924-3582
(Books)

## Trenton

Antiques by Selmon
10 Vetterlein Ave.
Trenton, NJ
(609) 586-0777

Armies of the Past Ltd.
2038 Greenwood Ave.
Trenton, NJ
(609) 890-0142

Ben's Used Furniture
112 N. Hermitage Ave.
Trenton, NJ
(609) 394-9024

Canty Inc.
1680 N. Olden Ave.
Trenton, NJ
(609) 530-1832

Searchmon
1027 S. Broad St.
Trenton, NJ
(609) 394-0099

# Middlesex County

Cranbury
Dayton
East Brunswick
Edison
Fords
Highland Park
Jamesburg
Metuchen
New Brunswick
North Brunswick
Pennington
Perth Amboy
Piscataway
Spotswood
Woodbridge

## Cranbury

Adams Brown Company
26 N. Main St.
Cranbury, NJ
(609) 655-8269
(By appointment only.)

Cranbury Book Worm
54 N. Main St.
Cranbury, NJ
(609) 655-1063
(Books only)

Anthony's Cranbury Antiques
60 N. Main St.
Cranbury, NJ
(609) 655-3777

David Wells Antiques
60 N Main St.
Cranbury, NJ
(609) 655-0085

## Dayton

Nannie's Pretties Antiques
425 Ridge Rd.
Dayton, NJ
(732) 329-2062

## East Brunswick

Heart & Soul Resale Emporium
204 Rt.18
East Brunswick, NJ
(732) 249-8050

LB Military Goods & Antiques
290 Rt.18
East Brunswick, NJ
(732) 238-6011

## Edison

Edison Hall Books
5 Ventnor Dr.
Edison, NJ
(732) 548-4455
(Books only, by appointment.)

## Fords

Bargain Market
491 New Brunswick Ave.
Fords, NJ
(732) 738-5077

## Highland Park

Karwen's Antiques
68 Raritan Ave.
Highland Park, NJ
(732) 828-5575

Rutgers Gun Center
127 Raritan Ave.
Highland Park, NJ
(732) 545-4344

Neil's Classic Novelty Emporium
179 Woodbridge Ave.
Highland Park, NJ
(732) 572-3286

# Jamesburg

Barbara's Unique Antique Boutique
35 E. Railroad Ave.
Jamesburg, NJ
(732) 521-9055

Leslie's Emporium
454 Spotswood-Englishtown Rd.
Jamesburg, NJ
(732) 251-0306

# Metuchen

Boro Art Center
505 Middlesex Ave.
Metuchen, NJ
(732) 549-7878

Round Trip Collectibles
9-B Pennsylvania Ave.
Metuchen, NJ
(732) 548-0082

Metuchen Antique Shop
267 Central Ave.
Metuchen, NJ
(732) 603-9724

# New Brunswick

Aaron Aardvark & Son
119 French St.
New Brunswick, NJ
(732) 246-1720

French Street Antiques
108 French St.
New Brunswick, NJ
(732) 545-9352

Amber Lion Antiques
365 George St. & Paterson St.
New Brunswick, NJ
(732) 214-9090

Gallen Furniture
162 Church St.
New Brunswick, NJ
(732) 846-3695

American Antiques Auction
1050 George St.
New Brunswick, NJ
(732) 247-6767

Somewhere In Time
115 French St.
New Brunswick, NJ
(732) 247-3636

# North Brunswick

Davidson Mill Village
2430 Rt. 130
North Brunswick, NJ
(732) 940-8600

# Pennington

S&S Collectibles
2516 Pennington Rd.
Pennington, NJ
(609) 737-3040
(By Appointment)

## Perth Amboy

Crystal Shoppe Antiques
289 High St.
Perth Amboy, NJ
(732) 442-2704

New Jersey Wholsale
450 Market St.
Perth Amboy, NJ
(732) 442-4242
(Reproductions)

Maid of Perth
211 Front St.
Perth Amboy, NJ
(732) 442-4472

## Piscataway

Becky's Antiques
500 New Market Rd.
Piscataway, NJ
(732) 968-6227

Metlar/Bodine House
1281 River Rd.
Piscataway, NJ
(732) 442-8366

## Spotswood

The Antique Shoppe
482 Main St.
Spotswood, NJ
(732) 251-9502

## Woodbridge

Nana's Attic
114 Main St.
Woodbridge, NJ
(732) 855-1121

# Monmouth County

Allentown

Allenwood

Asbury Park

Atlantic Highlands

Avon By The Sea

Belford

Belmar

Bradley Beach

Brielle

Colts Neck

Deal

Eatontown

Englishtown

Fair Haven

Farmingdale

Freehold

Highlands

Holmdel

Howell

Keyport

Little Silver

Locust

Long Branch

Manalapan

Manasquan

Marlboro

Middletown

Millstone

Navesink

Ocean Grove

Red Bank

Rumson

Sea Girt

Shrewsbury

South Belmar

Spring Lake

Wall

Wanamassa

West Belmar

West End

# Allentown

Brown Bear's Antiques
35 South Main St. (Corner of Lakeview
& S. Main)
Allentown, NJ
(609) 259-0177

Mill House Antiques
38 S. Main St.
Allentown, NJ
(609) 259-0659

# Allenwood

Allenwood General Store
Allenwood-Lakewood Rd.
Allenwood, NJ
(732) 223-0659

# Asbury Park

Ann Tiques
1022 Main St.
Asbury Park, NJ
(732) 869-0347

Past To Present
1024 Main St.
Asbury Park, NJ
(732) 774-5721

House of Modern Living
701 Cookman Ave.
Asbury Park, NJ
(732) 988-2350

Wm. Barron Galleries
504 Main St.
Asbury Park, NJ
(732) 988-7711
(Call for auction dates & times.)

Of Rare Vintage
718 Cookman Ave.
Asbury Park, NJ
(732) 988-9459

Olde England Antiques/Paul Mitchell
    Antiques
901 Main St. (Corner of 1st Ave. )
Asbury Park, NJ
(732) 988-6686/998-6686

# Atlantic Highlands

East House Antiques
Rt. 36 & Sears Ave.
Atlantic Highlands, NJ
(732) 291-2147

Treasure Cove Of Old
139 First Ave.
Atlantic Highlands, NJ
(732) 291-2078

# Avon By The Sea

Country By the Sea
515 Sylvania Ave.
Avon By The Sea, NJ
(732) 776-6671

# Belford

Mustillo & Sons
784 Rt. 36
Belford, NJ
(732) 787-1708

# Belmar

The Antique Connection
404 5th Ave.
Belmar, NJ
(732) 681-3970

# Bradley Beach

Touch of the Past
14 Main St.
Bradley Beach, NJ
(732) 988-1829

# Brielle

Brielle Antique Center
at Historic Union Landing
(Union & Green Lanes at the River)
Brielle, NJ
(732) 528-8570

Escargot Books
503 Rt. 71
Brielle, NJ
(732) 528-5955
(Books only)

Chappie's Antiques & Collectibles
406 Higgins Ave.
Brielle, NJ
(732) 528-8989

Relics
605-R Rt. 71
Brielle, NJ
(732) 223-3452

Country Cottage Antiques
709 Riverview Dr.
Brielle, NJ
(732) 528-9498

# Colts Neck

Goss Fine Arts
Artisan Way & Rt. 34
Colts Neck, NJ
(732) 431-4919

# Deal

Surrey Lane Antiques
Footnotes Plaza
280 Norwood Ave.
Deal, NJ
(732) 531-6991

# Eatontown

Earth Treasures & Jewelers
Office Max Plaza
Between Rt. 35 S & 36 W
Eatontown, NJ
(732) 542-5444
(Jewelry)

# Englishtown

Englishtown Auction Sales & Flea
  Market
Old Bridge Rd.
Englishtown, NJ
(908) 446-9644
(40 acres of indoor & outdoor stalls,
  over 1,000 dealers.)

Englishtown Antiques & Used
  Furniture
42 Main St.
Englishtown, NJ
(732) 446-3330

Mid-Jersey Antiquarian Book Center
480 Rt. 33
Englishtown, NJ
(732) 446-5656

# Fair Haven

Blue Stove Antiques
769 River Rd.
Fair Haven, NJ
(732) 747-6777

# Farmingdale

A Touch of Age
58A Main St.
Farmingdale, NJ
(732) 938-4064

Cobwebs Cottage
58 Main St. (Rts. 524 & 547)
Farmingdale, NJ
(732) 938-2626

# Freehold

County Seat Antique Center
28 W. Main St.
Freehold, NJ
(732) 431-2644
(38 dealers)

Frantiques
33 W. Main St.
Freehold, NJ
(732) 780-8872
(6 dealers)

Freehold Antique Gallery
21 W. Main St.
Freehold, NJ
(732) 462-7900
(50 dealers)

Freehold Furniture Exchange
2 Monmouth Ave.
Freehold, NJ
(732) 462-1333

Laura's Doll Houses & Collectibles
103 Koster Dr.
Freehold, NJ
(732) 294-7407

# Highlands

Forever Antiques
20 Bay Ave.
Highlands, NJ
(732) 872-6200

Suzanne's Antiques
2 Portland Rd.
Highlands, NJ
(732) 872-2881

# Holmdel

Raritan Bay Auction Services
26-A Van Brackle Rd.
Holmdel, NJ
(732) 264-6532
(Auctions held on Rt. 34 in Matawan.
   Call for dates & times.)

# Howell

Gemco Gold Buying Service
4335 Rt. 9
Howell, NJ
(732) 370-1959

Gemini Antiques
In Collingswood Flea Market
Collingswood Auction
Howell, NJ
(732) 938-4441

Haas Cienda Antiques
2301 Rt. 9N.
Howell, NJ
(732) 866-4484

Hidden Treasures Inc.
2301 Rt. 9
Howell, NJ
(732) 308-4414

Howell Station Antique Mall & Flea
   Market
2301 Rt. 9 N
Howell, NJ
(732) 308-1105

Katarina's Antiques
In Collingswood Flea Market
Rt. 33
Howell, NJ
(732) 938-4170

# Keyport

Collector's Cottage
34 Main St.
Keyport, NJ
(732) 264-2453

Front Porch Emporium
W. Front St.
Keyport, NJ
(732) 335-0826

Grandma's Olde & New Shoppe
34 W. Front St.
Keyport, NJ
(732) 335-4190

Keyport Antique Emporium
46-52 W. Front St.
Keyport, NJ
(732) 888-2952

Keyport Antique Market
W. Front St.
In the J. J. Newberry Bldg.
Keyport, NJ
(732) 203-1001

Keyport Consignment Shop
242 Broad St.
Keyport, NJ
(732) 739-4626

King's Treasures
29 W. Front St.
Keyport, NJ
(732) 335-8822

North River Antiques
2 W Front St.
Keyport, NJ
(732) 264-0580

Second Hand Lil
24 Broad St.
Keyport, NJ
(732) 264-0777

Second Hand Prose
8 Main St.
Keyport, NJ
(732) 335-9090
(Books)

Twice is Nice
24 W. Front St.
Keyport, NJ
(732) 888-9596

Upstairs Thrift Shop
12 Broad St.
Keyport, NJ
(732) 264-8043

## Little Silver

Mill House Antiques
32 Willow Dr.
Little Silver, NJ
(732) 741-7411

## Locust

Locust Antiques
487 Locust Point Rd.
Locust, NJ
(732) 291-4575

## Long Branch

Antiques by John Gormley
269 Broadway Ave.
Long Branch, NJ
(732) 571-4849/244-7724

Atlantic Antiques Inc.
267 Broadway Ave.
Long Branch, NJ
(732) 571-4919

Blue Cow Antiques
194 Westwood Ave.
Long Branch, NJ
(732) 747-7738

Hy'Spot Antiques & Collectibles
61 Brighton Ave.
Long Branch, NJ
(732) 222-7880

Stan Buck Restorations & Antiques
553 Broadway
Long Branch, NJ
(908) 229-0522

Take A Gander
84 Brighton Ave.
Long Branch, NJ
(732) 229-7389

## Manalapan

NJ Galleries
161 Pension Rd.
Manalapan Township, NJ
(732) 446-9490

# Manasquan

Carriage House Antique Center
140 Main St.
Manasquan, NJ
(732) 528-6772

Casey's Alley
73 Main St. & South Street Plaza
Manasquan, NJ
(908) 223-0064

Pot of Gold Antiques
2383 Ramshorn Dr.
Manasquan, NJ
(732) 528-6648
(By appointment)

# Marlboro

Grandma's Treasures
35 N. Main St.
Marlboro, NJ
(732) 462-2381

Marlboro Country Antiques
233 Rt. 79
Marlboro Township, NJ
(732) 946-8794

# Middletown

A Paradiso Garden
212 Rt. 35
Middletown Township, NJ
(732) 758-1340

# Millstone

Mid Jersey Antiquarian Book Center
480 Rt. 33
Millstone, NJ
(732) 446-5656
(Books only)

# Navesink

Locust Antiques
487 Locust Point Rd.
Navesink, NJ
(732) 291-4575

# Ocean Grove

Antic Hay Rare Books
45 Pilgrim Pathway
Ocean Grove, NJ
(732) 774-4590
(Books only)

# Red Bank

Antiques Associates
205 W. Front St.
Red Bank, NJ
(732) 219-0377

Antique Gallery
27 Monmouth St.
Red Bank, NJ
(732) 714-9296/224-0033

Aunt E's Attic
30 Monmouth St.
Red Bank, NJ
(732) 842-3651

British Cottage Antiques
126 Shrewsbury Ave.
Red Bank, NJ
(732) 530-0685

Cool Carousel
26 Broad St.
Red Bank, NJ
(732) 758-1700

Copper Kettle Antiques
15 Broad St.
Red Bank, NJ
(732) 741-8583

Double Dutch Antiques
18 Wallace St.
Red Bank, NJ
(732) 345-0845

Galleria Antiques
Bridge Ave. & W. Front St.
Red Bank, NJ
(732) 530-7300

Gaslight Antiques
212 W. Front St.
Red Bank, NJ
(732) 741-7323

Lone Arranger Outlet Store
101 Shrewsbury Rd.
Red Bank, NJ
(732) 747-9238

Mayfair House
60 Monmouth St.
Red Bank, NJ
(732) 219-8955

Monmouth Antique Shoppes
217 W. Front St.
Red Bank, NJ
(732) 842-7377

Plum Cottage
Riverside Dr. & Allen Place
Red Bank, NJ
(732) 219-5044

Riverbank Antiques & Interiors
169 W. Front St.
Red Bank, NJ
(732) 842-5400

Tea & Vintage
16 W. Front St.
Red Bank, NJ
(732) 741-6676

The Antiques Center of Red Bank
in three buildings:

Building I
195B W. Front St
(732) 741-5331

The Antiques Center-Building II
195 W. Front St.
(732) 842-3393

The Antiques Center-Building III
226 W. Front St.
Red Bank, NJ
(732) 842-4336

The Art & Attic
12 Broad St.
Red Bank, NJ
(732) 747-7007

T Berry Square
8 Broad St.
Red Bank, NJ
(732) 576-1819

Tower Hill Antiques & Design
147 Broad St.
Red Bank, NJ
(732) 842-5551

Two Broad Antiques
160 Monmouth Rd.
Red Bank, NJ
(732) 224-0122

Used Furniture Center of Red Bank
197 Shrewsbury Ave.
Red Bank, NJ
(732) 842-1449

Wild Flower Antiques
19 N. Bridge Ave. (Off W. Front)
Red Bank, NJ
(732) 933-7733

## Rumson

Eclectica
113 E. River Rd.
Rumson, NJ
(732) 758-8040

Mary Jane Roosevelt Antiques
109 E. River Rd.
Rumson, NJ
(732) 842-3159

## Sea Girt

H.E.Y. Enterprises
2100 Rt. 35, #26A
Sea Girt, NJ
(732) 974-8855
(Book only)

## Shrewsbury

Paris to Provence
655 Broad St.
Shrewsbury, NJ
(732) 747-6200

## South Belmar

Aajeda Antiques
1800 F St.
Corner of 18th & Main Sts.
S. Belmawr, NJ
(732) 681-2288

## Spring Lake

A Touch of the Past Antiques
410 Rt. 71
Spring Lake Heights, NJ
(732) 974-9200

Spring Lake Antiques
1201 3rd Ave.
Spring Lake, NJ
(732) 449-3322

Gallery III Antiques
1720 Rt. 71
Spring Lake Heights, NJ
(732) 449-7560

Vitale & Vitale Museum Gallery
315 Morris Ave.
Spring Lake, NJ
(732) 449-3000

Randolph Galleries
500 Rt. 71
Spring Lake Heights, NJ
(732) 974-0640

## Wall

Pot O Gold Antiques
2383 Ramshorn Dr. (Off Rt. 34)
South Wall, NJ
(732) 528-6648
(By appointment.)

# Wanamassa

About Time
1411 Wickapecko Drive
Wanamassa, NJ
(732) 775-4650
(clocks)

# West Belmar

Belmar Trading Post
1735 Rt. 71
W. Belmar, NJ
(732) 681-3207

# West End

Antiques & Accents
55 Brighton Ave.
West End, NJ
(732) 222-2274

Mother
61 Brigthon Ave.
West End, NJ
(732) 222-6469

# Morris County

Boonton
Butler
Cedar Knolls
Chatham
Chester
Denville
Dover
East Hanover
Kenvil
Long Valley
Madison
Mendham
Myersville
Millington
Morristown
Netcong
Newfoundland
Parsippany
Pine Brook
Pompton Plains
Randolph
Rockaway
Roxbury
Stirling
Towaco

# Boonton

Blue Shutters Antiques & Lamp
  Hospital
321 Main St.
Boonton, NJ
(973) 299-1344

Boonton Antiques/Antique Buying
  Associates
521 Main St.
Boonton, NJ
(973) 334-4416

Claire Ann's Antiques
815 Main St.
Boonton, NJ
(973) 334-2421

Carl's Antiques
904 Main St.
Boonton, NJ
(973) 263-9162

Fox Hill Exchange
900 Main St.
Boonton, NJ
(973) 263-2270

Old Feedmill Auction
487 Division St.
Boonton, NJ
(973) 334-0001
(Auctions every Friday)

Orange Poppy Antiques
413 Main St.
Boonton, NJ
(973) 263-1016

Remembrance of Things Past
315 Main St.
Boonton, NJ
(973) 402-9421

The Brass Connection
406 Main St.
Boonton, NJ
(973) 334-1424

The Cupboard Antiques
410 Main St.
Boonton, NJ
(973) 402-0400

The Shed Antique Furniture &
  Collectables
408 Main St.
Boonton, NJ
(973) 334-3686

The Tyndal Collections
920 Main St.
Boonton, NJ
(973) 334-3124

# Butler

CJ's Craft Cottage
7 High St.
Butler, NJ
(973) 492-0201

# Cedar Knolls

Antique Buying Addition
Morris County Mall & Ridgeway Ave.
Cedar Knoll, NJ
(973) 539-7840

# Chatham

Antique Buying Annex
1 N. Passaic Ave.
Chatham, NJ
(973) 635-2733

# Chester

Aunt Pittypats Parlour
57 E. Main St.
Chester, NJ
(908) 879-4253

Black River Trading Company
15 Perry St.
Chester, NJ
(908) 879-6778

Chester Antique Center
32 Grove St.
Chester, NJ
(908) 879-4331

Chester Carousel
125 Main St.
Chester, NJ
(908) 879-7141

Chester House
294 E. Main St.
Chester, NJ
(908) 879-7856

Doll Hospital
75 Main St.
Chester, NJ
(908) 879-4101

Doug's Antiques
87 W. Main St.
Chester, NJ
(908) 879-8088

Gingerbread Cottage Antiques
35 Perry St.
Chester, NJ
(908) 879-1164

Great American Country
25 Main St.
Chester, NJ
(908) 879-7797

Jantiques
10 Budd Ave.
Chester, NJ
(908) 879-9409

Marita Daniels Antiques
127 E. Main St.
Chester, NJ
(908) 879-6488

Once Upon A Time
32 Grove St.
Chester, NJ
(908) 879-4957

Pegasus Antiques
98 W. Main St.
Chester, NJ
(908) 879-4792

Robins Nest
125 Maple Ave.
Chester, NJ
(908) 879-5131

Spinning Wheel Antiques
76 E. Main St.
Chester, NJ
(908) 879-6080

Summerfield's Antique Furniture
44 Main St.
Chester, NJ
(908) 879-9020

The Beauty of Civilization Vintage
   Boutique
Perry St.
Chester, NJ
(908) 879-2044

The Chester Timepiece
58 Main St.
Chester, NJ
(908) 879-5421

The Emporium
71 Main St.
Chester, NJ
(908) 879-7751

The Postage Stamp
36 W. Main St.
Chester, NJ
(908) 879-4257

# Denville

Young's Antiques
78 Diamond Spring Rd.
Denville, NJ
(973) 625-0069
(By appointment)

# Dover

Azizifacts
1-5 W. Blackwell St.
Dover, NJ
(973) 366-1440

Berman Auction Gallery
33 W. Blackwell St.
Dover, NJ
(973) 361-3110
(Auctions every Wed, 6:00.)

Cecil's
29 W. Blackwell St.
Dover, NJ
(973) 442-8300

Duck's Traders In Fine Antiques
1 W. Blackwell St.
Dover, NJ
(973) 361-7579

Iron Carriage Antiques Center
1-5 Blackwell St.
Dover, NJ
(973) 366-1440
(40 dealers)

Peddler's Shop
71 W. Blackwell St.
Dover, NJ
(973) 361-0545

The Antique Jungle
12 W. Blackwell St.
Dover, NJ
(973) 537-0099

# East Hanover

All Things Consignment Antiques &
    Collectibles
159 Mt. Pleasant Ave.
East Hanover Township, NJ
(973) 428-0092

# Kenvil

Country Rooster
438 Rt. 46
Kenvil, NJ
(973) 584-2874

# Long Valley

German Valley Antiques
6 E. Mill Rd.
Long Valley, NJ
(908) 876-9202

Tavern Antiques
5 W. Mill Rd.
Long Valley, NJ
(908) 876-5854

Ye Olde Ballantine Village
20 Schooley's Mountain Rd.
Long Valley, NJ
(908) 876-4255

# Madison

New Lease Consignment Boutique
16 Park Ave.
Madison, NJ
(973) 377-2422

Rose's Closet
4 Lincoln Place
Madison, NJ
(973) 377-7673

Shug's Shop
14 Prospect St.
Madison, NJ
(973) 514-5955

The Chatham Bookseller
8 Green Village Rd.
Madison, NJ
(973) 822-1361
(Books only)

Threadneedle Street
Waverly Place
Madison, NJ
(973) 765-0360

Time After Time Vintage Clothing
81 Main St.
Madison, NJ
(973) 966-6877

The Ivy Porch
250 Main St.
Madison, NJ
(973) 514-1776

# Mendham

Antique Chair Shoppe
6 Hilltop Rd.
Mendham, NJ
(973) 543-2164

Diane Smith Quality Consignments
1 Hilltop Rd.
Mendham, NJ
(973) 543-6199

Grand Bazaar
13 E. Main St.
Mendham, NJ
(973) 543-4115

Painted Pony Antiques
16 W. Main St.
Mendham, NJ
(973) 543-6484

The Acorn Shop
6 Hilltop Rd.
Mendham, NJ
(973) 543-5914

# Meyersville

Archie's Resale Shop
596 Meyerville Rd.
Meyersville, NJ
(908) 647-1149

The Trading Post Antiquities
211 Hickory Tavern Rd.
Meyersville, NJ
(908) 647-1959

# Millington

Lou Souders-A Country Store
1901 Long Hill Rd.
Millington, NJ
(908) 647-7429

# Morristown

Coletree Antiques & Interiors
166 South St.
Morristown, NJ
(973) 993-3011

Fearless Fearick's Fabulous Furniture
166 Ridgedale Ave.
Morristown, NJ
(973) 984-3140

Jeffrey Eger
42 Blackberry Lane
Morristown, NJ
(973) 455-1843
(Books only, by appt. & mail order.)

Marion Jaye Antiques
990 Mt. Kemble Ave.
Morristown, NJ
(973) 425-0441

Morristown Antique Center
45 Market St. (Rt. 202)
Morristown, NJ
(973) 734-0900
(100 dealers.)

Old Book Shop
4 John St.
Morristown, NJ
(973) 538-1210
(Books, postcards, paper)

Robert Fountain Antiques
1107 Mt. Kemble Ave.
Morristown, NJ
(973) 425-8111

Rose Trellis
Mt. Kemble Ave. (Rt. 202)
Morristown, NJ
(973) 425-1192

The Cottage On The Country Mile
1001 Rt. 202
Morristown, NJ
(973) 425-0101

# Netcong

New To You
1 Maple Ave.
Netcong, NJ
(973) 347-9000

# Newfoundland

Antiques By Zelda
2915 Rt. 23
Newfoundland, NJ
(973) 697-1110

Red Wheel Antiques
2775 Rt. 23
Newfoundland, NJ
(973) 697-6133

# Parsippany

About Books
6 Sand Hill Court
Parsippany, NJ
(201) 515-4591
(Books only)

# Pine Brook

Dutch Gables Antiques
58 Maple Ave.
Pine Brook, NJ
(973) 227-2803

## Pompton Plains

Arch Gallery
629 Rt. 23
Pompton Plains, NJ
(973) 835-5034

Wayside Antiques Shop
5 Jackson Ave.
Pompton Plains, NJ
(973) 839-8129

## Randolph

Country Cottage Books & Cookies, Inc.
425 Rt. 10 (East)
Randolph, NJ
(973) 361-6777
(Books only)

## Rockaway

Grandma's Attic Inc.
282 W. Main St.
Rockaway Boro, NJ
(973) 625-1156

## Roxbury

Country Rooster Antiques & Collectibles
438 Rt. 46
Roxbury Township, NJ
(973) 584-2874

## Stirling

The Restore
253 Main St.
Stirling, NJ
(908) 647-0613

## Towaco

The Gazebo Antiques
21 Brook Valley Rd.
Towaco, NJ
(973) 334-0361

# Ocean County

Barnegat
Barnegat Light
Bay Head
Bayville
Beach Haven
Beach Haven Crest
Beachwood
Brick
Cedar Run
Eagleswood Township
Forked River
Holland Park
Jackson
Lakehurst
Lavalette
Long Beach
Manahawkin
Manchester
Mayetta
New Egypt
Ocean
Point Pleasant
Point Pleasant Beach
Spray Beach
Surf City
Toms River
Tuckerton
Waretown
West Creek
Whiting

# Barnegat

Babe's In Barnegat
Shoppers Corner
349 S. Main St. (Rt. 9)
Barnegat, NJ
(609) 698-2223

Barnegat Antique Country
684 E. Bay Ave.
Barnegat, NJ
(609) 698-8967

Barnegat Antiques & Uniques
323 Rt. 9
Barnegat, NJ
(609) 660-1464

Del's Antiques & Collectibles
307 S. Main St.
Barnegat, NJ
(609) 660-1688

Federal House Antiques
719 W. Bay Ave.
Barnegat, NJ
(609) 698-5490

First National Antiques
708 W. Bay Ave. & Railroad Ave.
Barnegat, NJ
(609) 698-1413

Forget Me Not Shoppe
689 E. Bay Ave.
Barnegat, NJ
(609) 698-3107

Lavendar Hall (Formerly Main Street
South Shops)
289 Rt. 9 (South)
Barnegat, NJ
(609) 698-8126
(5 dealers)

Lindy's
360 Bay Ave. (Rt. 9)
Barnegat, NJ
(609) 698-2415

Sneak Box Antiques & Decoys
273 S. Main St.
Barnagat, NJ
(609) 698-8222

The Goldduster
695 E. Bay Ave.
Barnegat, NJ
(609) 698-2520

The Raintree Cottage
273 S. Main St.
Barnegat, NJ
(609) 660-0777

# Barnegat Light

Americana by the Seashore
604 Broadway
Barnegat Light, NJ
(609) 494-0656

Nichole's Antiques
410 Broadway
Barnegat Light, NJ
(609) 494-1557

The Sampler
708 Broadway
Barnagat Light, NJ
(609) 494-3493

# Bay Head

Dee's Antiques & Collectibles
70 Bridge Ave.
Bay Head, NJ
(732) 899-8400

Fables of Bay Head
410 Main Ave. (Rt. 35)
Bay Head, NJ
(732) 899-3633

# Bayville

Antigo Antiques
510 Rt. 9
Bayville, NJ
(732) 237-2767

# Beach Haven

Maureen's Antiques & Collectibles
2807 Long Beach Blvd.
Beach Haven Garden, NJ
(609) 492-0400

Somewhere In Time
202 Centre Ave.
Beach Haven, NJ
(609) 207-1221

Pink Petunia
216 S. Bay Ave.
Beach Haven
(609) 492-0023

Summerhouse
412 N. Bay Ave.
Beach Haven, NJ
(609) 492-6420

# Beach Haven Crest

Age of Antiquities
8013 Long Beach Blvd.
Beach Haven Crest, NJ
(609) 494-0735

Wizard of Odds Antiques
7601 Long Beach Blvd.
Beach Haven Crest, NJ
(609) 494-9384/494-4661

House of Seven Wonders
7600 Long Beach Blvd.
Beach Haven Crest, NJ
(609) 494-9673

# Beachwood

All Antiques Appreciated
118 Atlantic City Blvd.
Beachwood, NJ
(732) 818-7719

# Brick

Antique Pavilion
40 Rt. 549 (Brick blvd.)
Brick, NJ
(732) 864-1116

Lavendar Lane Antiques &
  Collectibles
538 Brick Tavern Rd.
Brick, NJ
(732) 785-2784

The Bargain Outlet
2104 Rt. 88
Brick, NJ
(732) 892-9007

# Cedar Run

Jo's Thrift Shop
Rt. 9 S.
Cedar Run, NJ
(609) 597-1700

# Eagleswood Township

Pine Barrens Antiques
476 Rt. 9S.
Eagleswood Township, NJ
(609) 597-9300

# Forked River

Victorian Charm Antiques, Gifts & Collectibles
202 Rt. 9 (Main St.)
Forked River, NJ
(609) 597-1122

# Holland Park

Neil's Classic Novelty Emporium
179 Woodbridge Ave.
Holland Park, NJ
(732) 572-3286

Rutgers Gun Center
127 Raritan Ave.
Holland Park, NJ
(732) 545-4344
(Guns & Swords)

# Jackson

Unlock The Past
959 W. Veterans Hwy.
Jackson, NJ
(732) 928-5600

The Used Furniture Warehouse
427 Whitesville Road
Jackson, NJ
(732) 370-5445

# Lakehurst

Good Old Times Antique Village
3086 Rt. 571
Lakehurst, NJ
(732) 657-4433

Treasure Chest
666 Rt. 70 W
Lakehurst, NJ
(908) 657-2590

The Corner Shoppe
Rt. 571 & Rt. 70
Lakehurst, NJ
(732) 657-7127

# Lavalette

Clem's Antiques & Collectibles
1501 Rt. 35
Lavalette, NJ
(732) 793-2299

# Long Beach

Ship Bottom Antiques
Central Ave. at 28th St.
Long Beach Island, NJ
(609) 361-0885

# Manahawkin

Cornucopia
140 N. Main St. (Old Rt. 9)
Manahawkin, NJ
(609) 978-0099

Manor House Shops
160 N. Main St. (Rt. 9)
Manahawkin, NJ
(609) 597-1122

The Shoppes at Rosewood
182 N. Main St. (Rt. 9)
Manahawkin, NJ
(609) 597-7331

# Manchester

Calico Co-op
Good Old Time Village
Rt. 571 & 70
Manchester Township, NJ
(732) 657-8302

Old Ivy
3086 Rt. 571
Manchester Township, NJ
(732) 657-6490

# Mayetta

Country Charm Shoppes
775 S. Main St. (Rt. 9)
Mayetta, NJ
(609) 978-1737

# New Egypt

New Egypt Auction & Farmers
   Market
933 Rt. 537
New Egypt, NJ
(609) 758-2082
(Morning market & auction Sunday &
   Wed.)

Step Back In Time
45 Main St.
New Egypt, NJ
(609) 758-9598

Red Barn Antiques
56 Maple Ave.
New Egypt, NJ
800-400-8765/(609) 758-9152

# Ocean

White Elephant Garage Sale Bar & Grill
1500 Rt. 35
Ocean Township, NJ
(732) 517-0619

# Point Pleasant

Backstreet Antiques
1000 Trenton Ave. (Corner of Arnold
    Ave.)
Point Pleasant, NJ
(732) 714-9296

Concepts I Auction House, Inc.
1125 Arnold Ave.
Point Pleasant, NJ
(732) 892-6040

Pomegranate/The Acquisitive Eye
707 Arnold Ave.
Point Pleasant, NJ
(732) 892-0200

# Point Pleasant Beach

Antiques Etc.
1225 Bay Ave.
Point Pleasant Beach, NJ
(732) 295-9888

Book Bin
725 Arnold Ave.
Point Pleasant Beach, NJ
(732) 892-3456
(Books only.)

Classy Collectibles
633 Arnold Ave.
Point Pleasant Beach, NJ
(732) 714-0957

Feather Tree Antiques
624 Bay Ave.
Point Pleasant Beach, NJ
(732) 899-8891

Fond Memories Antiques
625-R Arnold Ave.
Point Pleasant Beach, NJ
(732) 892-4149

Globetrotter
(Seasonal Location)
1809 Ocean Ave.
Point Pleasant Beach, NJ
(732) 892-2001

Pleasant Times
626 Bay Ave.
Point Pleasant Beach, NJ
(732) 295-0005

Point Pleasant Antique Emporium
Corner of Bay Ave. & Trenton Ave.
Point Pleasant Beach, NJ
(732) 892-2222/800-322-8002
(Over 100 dealers)

Shore Antique Center
300 Richmond Ave. (Rt. 35 South)
Point Pleasant Beach, NJ
(732) 295-5771
(35 dealers)

The Clock & Antique Shop
726A Arnold Ave.
Point Pleasant Beach, NJ
(732) 899-6200

The Company Store
628 Bay Ave.
Point Pleasant Beach, NJ
(732) 892-5353
(8 dealers)

The Snow Goose
641 Arnold Ave.
Point Pleasant Beach, NJ
(732) 892-6929

The Time Machine
516 Arnold Ave.
Point Pleasant Beach, NJ
(732) 295-9695

Wally's Follies Antiques
626 Arnold Ave.
Point Pleasant Beach, NJ
(732) 899-1840

Willinger's Annex
626 Ocean Rd.
Point Pleasant Beach, NJ
(732) 892-2217
(30 dealers)

# Spray Beach

Remember Me Antiques
2611 Long Beach Blvd.
Spray Beach, NJ
(609) 492-7740

## Surf City

Court's Treasure Chest
1500 Long Beach Blvd.
Surf City, NJ
(609) 494-0910

Hill Galleries
1603 Long Beach Blvd.
Surf City, NJ
(609) 361-8225

## Toms River

Absolutely All Antiques
612 Helen St.
Toms River, NJ
(732) 240-2429

Main Street Antique Center
249-251 Main St.
Toms River, NJ
(732) 349-5764
(12 dealers)

All State Buyers, Inc.
#2 Rt. 37E
Toms River, NJ
(732) 244-5312

Priced Rite Used Furniture
98 Flint Rd.
S. Toms River, NJ
(732) 818-0007

Antique Outlet
552 Lakehurst Rd.
Toms River, NJ
(732) 286-7788

The Piggy Bank
2018 Rt. 37 (East)
Toms River, NJ
(732) 506-6133

Elizabeth Fischer
249 Main St.
Toms River, NJ
(732) 349-3863/244-3815

## Tuckerton

Consign/Design
147 E. Main St.
Tuckerton, NJ
(609) 978-2987

The Old Apple Tree Cottage Shoppes
130 S. Green St.
Tuckerton, NJ
(609) 294-1527

Country Corner Furniture
Rt. 9
Tuckerton, NJ
(609) 294-2606
(Used furniture outlet)

Tuckerton Emporium
2 East Main St. (Rt. 9)
Tuckerton, NJ
(609) 296-2424

## Waretown

Thrift Barn
Rt. 9
Waretown, NJ
(609) 693-6306

## West Creek

Helen's Antiques
662 Rt. 9
West Creek, NJ
(609) 660-1230

## Whiting

A Backward Glance
Rt. 530 W. & School House Rd.
Crestwood Shopping Plaza
Whiting, NJ
(732) 278-9453

# Passaic County

Bloomfield
Clifton
Passaic
Paterson
Pompton Lakes
West Milford

# Bloomfield

Grandma's Attic
174 1/2 Broad St.
Bloomfield, NJ
(973) 429-0121

## Clifton

Aladdin Thrift Shoppe
290 Parker Ave.
Clifton, NJ
(973) 773-9336

Granny's Attic
1080 Main St.
Clifton, NJ
(973) 772-1929
(Only open on Saturday.)

Antique Cottage Liquidators
35 Dermott Ave.
Clifton, NJ
(973) 472-4251

## Passaic

Jan, Jill & Jon
170 Main Ave.
Passaic, NJ
(973) 777-4670

Our Favorite Things
90 Dayton Ave.
Passaic, NJ
(973) 779-6997

## Paterson

Granny's Attic
Marion St.
Paterson, NJ
(201) 529-5516
(Only open Sat. & Sun., 11-5.)

Lucky Thrifts
245 Crooks St.
Paterson, NJ
(973) 684-4904

## Pompton Lakes

Carroll's Antiques
326 Wanaque Ave.
Pompton Lakes, NJ
(973) 831-6186

Pickers Paradise
269 Wanaque Ave.
Pompton Lakes, NJ
(973) 616-9500

Charisma 7 Antiques
326 Wanaque Ave.
Pompton Lakes, NJ
(973) 839-7779

Sterling Antique Center
222 Wanaque Ave.
Pompton Lakes, NJ
(973) 616-8986

PK's Treasures Ltd
229 Wanaque Ave.
Pompton Lakes, NJ
(973) 835-5212

## West Milford

C R C Auctioneers
1898 Macopin Rd.
West Milford, NJ
(973) 728-0201

# Salem County

**Alloway**
**Elmer**
**Monroeville**
**Pennsville**
**Sharptown**
**Woodstown**

# Alloway

Dorrell's Antiques
21 Lambert St.
Alloway, NJ
(609) 935-4296

Seven Hearths Antiques
34 N.Greenwich St.
Alloway, NJ
(609) 935-4976

# Elmer

George Hawriluk
Buck Rd.
Elmer, NJ
(609) 358-7267

Mullica Hill Art Glass
Rt. 40
Elmer, NJ
(609) 358-1200

# Monroeville

Elmer Auction Co.
260 Swedesboro Rd.
Monroeville, NJ
(609) 358-8433
(Call for auction dates & times.)

# Pennsville

Country Peddlar
104 N. Hook Rd.
Pennsville, NJ
(609) 678-5509

Holly Tree Antiques
101 William Penn Ave.
Pennsville, NJ
(609) 678-7100

# Sharptown

Cow Town Flea Market
Rt. 40
Sharptown, NJ
(609) 769-3202
(Indoor & outdoor flea market every
   Tuesday & Saturday.)

RanchoThrift Shop
Rt. 40
Sharptown, NJ
(609) 769-2394

Manor House Antiques
1099 Kings Hwy.
Sharptown, NJ
(609) 769-0766

# Woodstown

Oakbarn Antiques & Collectibles
At Victorian Rose Farm Bed &
   Breakfast
947 Rt. 40
Woodstown, NJ
(609) 769-4600
(A multi-dealer co-op.)

The American Country Shoppe
21 East Ave. (Rt. 45)
Woodstown, NJ
(609) 769-3800

# Somerset County

Bedminster
Belle Mead
Bernardsville
Bound Brook
Blawenburg
Bridgewater
East Millstone
Gladstone
Green Brook
Kingston
Martinsville
North Branch
North Plainfield
Peapack
Pluckemin
Raritan
Somerset
Somerville
Watchung

# Bedminster

Baobab Books
1555 Lamington Rd.
Bedminster, NJ
(908) 234-9163
(Books only, by appointment.)

Gypsy Caravan Antiques
364 Main St.
Bedminster, NJ
(908) 781-1600

Lamington General Store
Lamington Rd. (Rt. 523)
Bedminster, NJ
(908) 781-1600

Potters Shed Antiques
95 Sommerville Rd.
Bedminster, NJ
(908) 781-1935

# Belle Mead

Richard W. Cain Antiques
10 County Route 601
Belle Mead, NJ
(908) 359-5206

# Bernardsville

Bernardsville Antiques & Design
111 Morristown Rd.
Bernardsville, NJ
(908) 204-0868

Country Creations at Four Seasons of
    New Vernon
Rt. 202
Bernardsville, NJ
(201) 425-9310

Encore Quality Consignments
123A Claremont Rd.
Bernardsville, NJ
(908) 766-7760

Fred B. Nadler Antiques
27 Olcott Square
Bernardsville, NJ
(908) 766-6552

Peter Sena/Mine Brook Antiques
Rt. 202
Bernardsville, NJ
(908) 766-3505

The Country Sampler
Rt. 202
Bernardsville, NJ
(201) 425-1192

# Blawenburg

Decorators Consignment Gallery
Corner of Rts. 518 & 601(Elm or Great Rd.)
Blawenburg, NJ
(609) 466-4400

# Bound Brook

DiBetti Antiques
16 Hamilton St.
Bound Brook, NJ
(732) 356-3735

I Remember When
1 and 3 Maiden Lane
Bound Brook, NJ
(732) 563-1012

New Jersey Memories
401 E. Main St.
Bound Brook, NJ
(732) 560-0488

# Bridgewater

River Edge Farm Antiques
191 Church Rd.
(908) 722-3554
(By appointment.)

# East Millstone

Franklin Inn Bookstore
2371 Amwell Rd.
East Millstone, NJ
(908) 873-5344
(Books only)

# Gladstone

Thompson's Antiques
279 Main St.
Gladstone, NJ
(908) 719-2424

# Green Brook

Attic Treasures
319-323 Rt. 22
Green Brook, NJ
(732) 752-2442

# Kingston

Adorn Gallery
4422 Rt. 27
Kingston, NJ
(609) 683-7225

Quality Consignment
61 Main St.
Kingston, NJ
(609) 924-3924

Kingston Antiques/Dorothy
~ Oppenheim
4446 Rt. 27
Kingston, NJ
(609) 924-0332

# Martinsville

Martinsville Antique Center
1944 Washington Valley Rd.
Martinsville, NJ
(732) 302-1229
(10 dealers)

Mountain House
Martinsville Area, NJ
(732) 469-2195
(Oriental Porcelain, clocks & art glass,
    by appt.)

# North Branch

Little House Antiques
3355 Rt. 22 (East)
North Branch, NJ
(908) 526-6235

# North Plainfield

Collector's Corner
326 Somerset St.
North Plainfield, NJ
(908) 753-2650

# Peapack

Ludlow & Ely Antiques
151 Main St.
Peapak, NJ
(908) 781-6655

# Pluckemin

Country Antique Shop
Rts. 202 & 206
Pluckemin, NJ
(908) 658-3759

# Raritan

Towne Antiques
34 W. Somerset St.
Raritan, NJ
(908) 526-3455

Village Antiques
W. Somerset St.
Raritan, NJ
(908) 526-7920
(over 50 dealers)

# Somerset

Bill's Trading Post
459 Somerset St.
Somerset, NJ
(732) 247-4406

# Somerville

County Seat Antiques
41 W. Main St.
Somerville, NJ
(908) 595-9556

Somerville Antique Center
17 Division St.
Somerville, NJ
(908) 526-3446
(65 dealers)

D & D Galleries
Box 8413
Somerville, NJ
(908) 874-3162
(Books only, by appt.)

The Art Gallery Antiques
30 Division St.
Somerville, NJ
(908) 429-0370

Incogneeto Neet-O-Rama
19 W. Main St.
Somerville, NJ
(908) 231-1887

"Uptown " at Somerville Center
  Antiques
13 Division St.
Somerville, NJ
(908) 595-1294

P.M. Bookshop
59 W. Main St.
Somerville, NJ
(908) 722-0055
(Books only)

# Watchung

Valley Furniture Shop
20 Stirling Rd.
Watchung, NJ
(908) 756-7623
(Reproductions)

# Sussex County

Andover
Franklin
Hainesville
Lafayette
Montague
Newton
Sparta
Stanhope
Stillwater
Stockholm
Sussex
Vernon

# Andover

Andover Antiques
118 Rt. 206
Andover, NJ
(973) 786-5007/813-8782

Jay's Antiques
118 Rt. 206
Andover, NJ
(973) 786-5007

Andover Mixed Bag
Rt. 206
Andover, NJ
(973) 786-7702

Oriental Rugs & Antiques
Rt. 206
Andover, NJ
(973) 786-6004

Andover Village Shops
125 Main St.
Andover, NJ
(973) 786-6494

Scranberry Coop
42 Main St. (Rt. 206)
Andover, NJ
(973) 786-6414

Country and Stuff
127 Main St. (Rt. 206)
Andover, NJ
(973) 786-7086

Great Andover Antique Company
124 Main St. (Rt. 206)
Andover, NJ
(973) 786-6384
(15 dlrs.)

# Franklin

Edison Antiques Inc.
49 Church St. (County Rt. 631)
Franklin, NJ
(973) 827-7136

Munson Emporium
33 Munsonhurst Rd.
Franklin, NJ
(973) 827-0409

# Hainesville

Colophon Books
Ayers Rd.
Hainesville, NJ
(973) 948-5785
(Books only)

# Lafayette

Jim Bogwater Antiques
12 Morris Farm Rd.
Lafayette, NJ
(973) 383-6057/383-8170

Lafayette Mill Antique Center
12 Morris Farm Rd.
Lafayette, NJ
(973) 383-0065
(40 dealers)

Hartmann's Country Antiques
Corner of Rt. 15 & Morris Farm Rd.
Lafayette, NJ
(973) 300-0099

# Lafayette (continued)

Lamplighters of Lafayette
156 Rt. 15
Lafayette, NJ
(973) 383-5513

Sign of the Times
Morris Farm Rd.
Lafayette, NJ
(973) 383-6028

Lockward Antiques
102 Rt.15
Lafayette, NJ
(973) 383-1434

Silver Willow Inc.
Morris Farm Rd. & Rt. 15
Lafayette, NJ
(973) 383-5560

Mill Mercantile
11 Morris Farm Rd.
Lafayette, NJ
(973) 579-1588

Sweet Pea's
Morris Farm Rd.
Lafayette, NJ
(973) 579-6338

Pumleye's Antique Shop
Rt. 15
Lafayette, NJ
(973) 383-2114

Vermont Crossroads
Morris Farm Rd. & Rt. 15
Lafayette, NJ
(973) 383-6223

## Montague

Jean's Antiques
445 Rt. 206
Montague, NJ
(973) 293-7311/(800) 399-0409

## Newton

Irene M. Pavese
7 Main St.
Newton, NJ
(973) 579-6469

Second Chance
37 Miller Ave.
Newton, NJ
(973) 579-2028

North East Stained Glass Inc.
55 Mill St.
Newton, NJ
(973) 383-0006

The Galleria
132 Spring St.
Newton, NJ
(973) 383-8783

Nostalgia Shop
139 Spring St.
Newton, NJ
(973) 383-7233

## Sparta

Return Engagement
20 Main St.
Sparta, NJ
(973) 729-5515

Sparta Antiques Center
24 Main St.
Sparta, NJ
(973) 729-4545

# Stanhope

Stanhope Peddlars Village
149 Main St.
Stanhope, NJ
(908) 879-6676
(Call for auction dates & times.)

# Stillwater

Antiques & Collectibles
923 Main St.
Stillwater, NJ
(973) 579-9933

The Wooden Skate
903 Main St.
Stillwater, NJ
(973) 383-3094

# Stockholm

Red Wheel Antiques
2775 Rt. 23 S.
Stockholm, NJ
(973) 697-6133

Stockholm Antique Center
2841 Rt. 23 S.
Stockholm, NJ
(973) 697-9622

Snufftown Consignments
108 Rt. 23
Stockholm, NJ
(973) 208-0135

# Sussex

Clove Brook Antiques
761 Rt. 23
Sussex, NJ
(973) 702-7113

# Vernon

Antique Mania
399 Rt. 515
Vernon, NJ
(973) 764-6981

# Union County

**Cranford**
**Elizabeth**
**Garwood**
**Hillside**
**Linden**
**New Providence**
**Plainfield**
**Rahway**
**Roselle**
**Scotch Plains**
**Summit**
**Union**
**Westfield**

# Cranford

Cobweb Collectibles & Ephemera
9 Walnut Ave.
Cranford, NJ
(908) 272-5777

Dovetails
6 Eastman St.
Cranford, NJ
(908) 709-1638

Nancy's Antiques & 2nd Hand
  Furniture
7 Walnut Ave.
Cranford, NJ
(908) 272-5056

Not Just Antiques
218 South Avenue E
Cranford, NJ
(908) 276-3553

Shirley Green's Antiques
8 Eastman St.
Cranford, NJ
(908) 709-0066

# Elizabeth

E & E Antiques
10 Jefferson Ave.
Elizabeth, NJ
(908) 289-9293

G. Van Wolper Antiques
Elizabeth, NJ
(908) 354-8649
(French art glass by mail order)

Lotus Books
544 Linden Ave.
Elizabeth, NJ
(908) 354-7446
(Books only)

Union County Exchange
1173 Elizabeth Ave.
Elizabeth, NJ
(908) 353-6183

# Garwood

Classic Antiques
225 North Ave.
Garwood, NJ
(908) 233-7667

# Hillside

Turn of The Century Antiques
1538 Liberty Ave.
Hillside, NJ
(973) 318-7100

# Linden

Antiquities
523 Wood Ave.
Linden, NJ
(908) 925-1021

Time & Again
Route 1 & 9 North
1761 W. Edgar Rd.
Linden, NJ
(800) 290-5401/(908) 862-0200

Time & Again Antiques & Used
  Furniture
Rt. 109
Linden/Rahway border, NJ
(908) 352-6334

# New Providence

British Pine Emporium
1296 Springfield Ave.
New Providence, NJ
(908) 508-9272

Dot's Wot Not Shop
1788 Springfield Ave.
New Providence, NJ
(908) 464-3810

New Providence Antique Center
1283 Springfield Ave.
New Providence, NJ
(908) 464-9191

# Plainfield

Kenny's Used Furniture
300 W. Front St.
Plainfield, NJ
(908) 753-4474

Rosebud Antiques
519 Park Ave.
Plainfield, NJ
(908) 757-7000

Tierney's Antiques
515 Park Ave.
Plainfield, NJ
(908) 753-2417

Tony D's Used Furniture
414 Watchung Ave.
Plainfield, NJ
(908) 226-1025

# Rahway

Just About Anything
1540 Main St.
Rahway, NJ
(732) 381-5900

Ken's Antiques
1667 Irving St.
Rahway, NJ
(732) 381-7306

Old Serendipity Shop
690 W. Grand Ave.
Rahway, NJ
(732) 388-4393 \ 388-1265

Royal Treasures Antique Inc
65 E. Cherry St.
Rahway, NJ
(732) 827-0409
(By appointment)

Tarnished Swan
74 Cherry St. West
Rahway, NJ
(732) 499-7111

# Roselle

Dav-Lo's Treasure Hunt
119 Chestnut St.
Roselle, NJ
(908) 245-0599

Roselle Antique Center
Corner of 1st Ave. & Aldene Rd.
Roselle, NJ
(908) 241-9034

## Scotch Plains

Chem Clean Antiques, Furniture &
  Restorations
505 Terrill Rd. & East 2nd St.
Scotch Plains, NJ
(908) 322-4433

Heinmeyer's Collectible Antiques
  Records & Plants
1380 Terrill Rd.
Scotch Plains, NJ
(908) 322-1788

Heritage Antiques Center
364 Park Ave.
Scotch Plains, NJ
(908) 322-2311

Old Forge Pine
Park Ave. & Front St.
Scotch Plains, NJ
(908) 322-7085

Seymour's Antiques & Collectibles
  Div of Design Center of NJ, Inc.
1732 E. 2nd St.
Scotch Plains, NJ
(908) 322-1300

Stage House Village
Park Ave. & Front St.
Scotch Plains, NJ
(908) 322-9090

## Summit

Antiques & Art By The Conductor
88 Summit Ave.
Summit, NJ
(908) 273-6893

Charming Home
358 Springfield Ave.
Summit, NJ
(908) 598-1022

Consignment & Auction Galleries of
  Summit
83 Summit Ave.
Summit, NJ
(908) 273-5055
(Call for auction dates & times.)

Country House
361 Springfield Ave.
Summit, NJ
(908) 277-3400

Handmaids
37 Maple St.
Summit, NJ
(908) 273-0707

Plumquin
12 Beechwood Rd.
Summit, NJ
(908) 273-3425

Somerset Wicker
10 Beechwood Rd.
Summit, NJ
(908) 277-0448

Summit Antiques Center Inc.
511 Morris Ave.
Summit, NJ
(908) 273-9373
(50 dealers)

The Sampler
96 Summit Ave.
Summit, NJ
(908) 277-4747

The Second Hand
519 Morris Ave.
Summit, NJ
(908) 273-6021

The Summit Exchange
29 Lafayette Ave.
Summit, NJ
(908) 273-2867

# Union

Pastimes 'N Presents
1420 Burnet Ave.
Union, NJ
(908) 688-6335

Union Galleries
1330 Stuyvesant Ave.
Union, NJ
(908) 964-1440

The Lawbook Exchange, LTD.
965 Jefferson Ave.
Union, NJ
(908) 686-1998/ 800-422-6686
(Books only)

# Westfield

Back Room Antiques
39 Elm St.
Westfield, NJ
(908) 654-5777

South Avenue Antiques
433 South Ave.
Westfield, NJ
(908) 232-1444

Betty Gallagher Antiques Inc.
266 E. Broad St.
Westfield, NJ
(908) 654-4222

The Attic
415 Westfield Ave.
Westfield, NJ
(908) 233-1954

Linda Elmore Antiques
395 Cumberland St.
Westfield, NJ
(908) 233-5443

The Old Toy Shop
759 Central Ave.
Westfield, NJ
(908) 232-8388

MaryLou's Memorabilia
17 Elm St.
Westfield, NJ
(908) 654-7277

Westfield Antiques
510 Central Ave.
Westfield, NJ
(908) 232-3668

# Warren County

Belvidere
Broadway
Buttzville
Columbia
Hackettstown
Harmony
Hope
New Village
Oxford
Phillipsburg
Port Murray
Stewartsville
Washington

# Belvidere

H & H Liquidating Company
427 Mansfield St.
Belvidere, NJ
(908) 475-4333

The Painted Lady
16 Greenwich St.
Belvidere, NJ
(908) 475-1985

Major Hoops Emporium Antiques
13 Market St.
Belvidere, NJ
(908) 475-5031

Timeline & Co.
318 Water St.
Belvidere, NJ
(908) 475-5606

Second Hand Rose, Inc.
203 Washington Ave.
Belvidere, NJ
(201) 759-0019

Uncommon Market
228 Mansfield St.
Belvidere, NJ
(908) 475-1460

# Broadway

Herbalist & Achemist Books
Box 553
Broadway, NJ
(908) 835-0822
(Books by mail order only.)

# Buttzville

Buttzville Center
274 Rt. 46
Buttzville, NJ
(908) 453-2918

# Columbia

Randi Roleson Antiques
468 Rt. 94
Columbia, NJ
(908) 496-4610

# Hackettstown

Family Attic Antiques, Ltd.
117 Main St.
Hackettstown, NJ
(908) 852-1206

Hanna's Attic Antiques
11 Rt. 46 W
Hackettstown, NJ
(908) 852-9300

Furnishings By Adam
253 Main St.
Hackettstown, NJ
(908) 852-4385

Main Street Bazaar
128 Willow Grove St.
Hackettstown, NJ
(908) 813-2966

Gabriella's Garret
124 Main St.
Hackettstown, NJ
(908) 852-9696

Whispering Pines Antiques
1878 Rt. 57
Hackettstown, NJ
(908) 852-2587

# Harmony

Harmony Barn Antiques
2481 Belvidere Rd. (Rt. 519 N.)
Harmony Township, NJ
(908) 859-6159

# Hope

Wagon Wheel Antiques
420 Silver Lake Rd.
Hope, NJ
(908) 459-5392

# New Village

New Village
2503 Rt. 57
New Village, NJ
(908) 213-0242

# Oxford

Jack's Barn
Route 31
Oxford, NJ
(908) 453-3665

# Phillipsburg

David K. Campbell Antiques
103 Foch Blvd.
Phillipsburg, NJ
(908) 454-3982

Gracy's Manor
1400 Belvidere Rd.
Phillipsburg, NJ
(908) 859-0928

Michael J. Stasak Antiques
376 River Rd.
Phillipsburg, NJ
(908) 454-6136

The Trading Post Antique Shop
Still Valley Circle
Phillipsburg, NJ
(908) 454-6091

# Port Murray

Rocking Horse Antiques
501 Rt. 57
Port Murray, NJ
(908) 689-2813

Port Murray Emporium
174 Main St.
Port Murray, NJ
(908) 689-6797

# Stewartsville

1764 House
509 Uniontown Rd. (Rt. 519)
Stewartsville, NJ
(908) 859-1414

Fieldstone Antiques
646 S. Main St.
Stewartsville, NJ
(908) 454-7523
(By appt.)

Stone House Farm Antiques
Rt. 57
Stewartsville, NJ
(908) 213-1808

# Washington

Pieces of the Past Antiques
67 E. Washington Ave.
Washington, NJ
(908) 689-3536

The Oak Tree Antiques
169 E. Washington Ave.
Washington, NJ
(908) 689-3714

# Pennsylvania

**Berks County**
**Bucks County**
**Chester County**
**Delaware County**
**Lancaster County**
**Lehigh County**
**Montgomery County**
**Northampton County**
**Philadelphia County**

# Berks County

**Barto**
**Bernville**
**Boyertown**
**Douglassville**
**Fleetwood**
**Hamburg**
**Hereford**
**Kutztown**
**Lebanon**
**Leesport**
**Maxatawney**
**Morgantown**
**Oley**
**Pikeville**
**Reading**
**Shartlesville**
**Sinking Spring**

## Barto

Terry L. Dwyer
164 Old Company Rd.
Barto, PA
(215) 679-5036

## Bernville

Yesteryear's
4th St. (Rt. 183)
Bernville, PA
(610) 488-0232

## Boyertown

Boyertown Antiques
1283 Weisstown Rd.
Boyertown, PA
(610) 367-2452

The Twin Turrets Inn
11 E. Philadelphia Ave.
Boyertown, PA
(610) 367-45113

Greshville Antiques
1041 Reading Rd.
Boyertown, PA
(610) 367-0076

## Douglassville

Stepp's Antiques
1528 Weavertown Road
Douglassville, PA
(610) 582-5918

Amity House of Antiques & Custom
  Framing
1143 Old Swede Road
Douglassville, PA
(610) 689-8626
(By appointment only.)

Merritt's Antiques Inc.
1860 Weavertown Rd.
Douglassville, PA
(610) 689-9541

## Fleetwood

Antique Complex of Fleetwood I
On Rt. 222
Fleetwood, PA
(610) 994-0707

Antique Complex of Fleetwood II
On Rt. 222
Fleetwood, PA
(610) 944-0707

## Hamburg

Jean's Vintage Textiles
342 3rd St.
Hamburg, PA
(717) 733-2252

# Hereford

Phil's Used Furniture & Antiques
Rts. 29 & 100
Hereford, PA
(215) 679-8625

# Kutztown

Antiques at Irene Bier's
164 Main St.
Kutztown, PA
(610) 395-6204

Kutztown Art Glass Gallery
230 Noble St.
Kutztown, PA
(610) 683-5714

Baver's Antiques
232 W. Main St.
Kutztown, PA
(610) 683-5045

Louise's Old Things
163 W. Main St.
Kutztown, PA
(610) 683-8370

Colonial Shop
224 W. Main St.
Kutztown, PA
(610) 683-3744
(By appointment)

Renninger's Antiques & Collectors
   Markets II
Noble St.
Kutztown, PA
(610) 683-6848/717-385-0104

Greenwich Mills
1097 Krumsville Rd.
Kutztown, PA
(610) 683-7866

# Lebanon

Serendipity Antique Barn
2799 E. Cumberland St.
Lebanon, PA
(717) 274-2799

# Leesport

Leesport Antique Mart
162 Center Ave. (Rt. 61)
Leesport, PA
(610) 926-2019

# Maxatawny

Antiques Etc.
15878 Kutztown Rd.
Maxatawny, PA
(610) 683-8834

Yesterday's Memories Antiques
Rt. 222
Maxatawny, PA
(610) 683-5657

# Morgantown

The Mill Property
Exit 22 PA Turnpike
W. Main St. (Rt. 23)
Morgantown, PA
(610) 286-8854
(90 dealers.)

The Antique Connection
238 W. Main St. (Rt. 23)
Morgantown, PA
(610) 286-4785

Treasure Hill Antiques
W. Main St. (Rt. 23)
Morgantown, PA
(610) 286-7119

Wrights Auction
Rts. 10 & 23
Morgantown, PA
(610) 286-0555
(Auctions every Wed. evening, 5:30.)

# Oley

Oley Valley Auction Co.
Rt. 73 & Oley Rd.
Oley , PA
(610) 987-9080

Oley Valley Reproductions
6321 Oley Turnpike Rd.
Oley, PA
(610) 689-5885
(American Period formal & country
    reproductions.)

# Pikeville

Pikeville Antiques
Oysterdale Rd.
Pikeville, PA
(610) 987-6635

# Reading

Cook's Antiques
147 Sycamore Rd.
Reading, PA
(610) 372-1681

Green Hills Auction Center
1540 New Holland Rd.
Reading, PA
(610) 775-2000
(Auctions every Monday.)

Memories
622 Penn Ave.
West Reading, PA
(610) 374-4480
(Vintage clothing & jewelry)

Ocasio Used Furniture & Second
    Hand Store
312 N. 9th St.
Reading, PA
(610) 375-7896

Pennypacker-Andrews Auction
    Centre Inc.
1530 New Holland Rd. (Rt. 222)
Reading, PA
(610) 777-6121
(Auctions held in Gouglersville.
    Call for dates.)

Ray's Antiques & Refinishing
401 N. 5th St.
Reading, PA
(610) 373-2907

Sylvia Christy Antiques
1008 Penn St.
Reading, PA
(610) 478-0599

The Christy Collection
1015 Penn St.
Reading, PA
(610) 375-4060

# Reading (continued)

Weaver Antique Mall
3730 Lancaster Pike (Rt. 222)
Reading, PA
(610) 777-8535

White's Store Front
304 N. 5th St.
Reading, PA
(610) 374-8128

## Shartlesville

Antique Treasures
Roadside Dr.
Shartlesville, PA
(610) 488-1545

Heritage Quilts & Antiques
3rd & Main Sts.
Shartlesville, PA
(610) 488-0808

## Sinking Spring

Alternative Furnishings
3728 Lancaster Pike (Rt. 422)
Sinking Spring, PA
(610) 796-2990

Zerbes' Auction Center
138 Wheatfield Rd.
Sinking Spring, PA
(610) 678-6685
(Auctions every Thursday evening.)

# Bucks County

Andalusia

Bensalem

Blooming Glen

Bristol

Buckingham

Carversville

Chalfont

Cornwells Heights

Doylestown

Dublin

Feasterville

Forest Grove

Fountainville

Furlong

Gardenville

Holicong

Hulmeville

Ivyland

Lahaska

Langhorne

Levittown

Lumberville

Mechanicsville

Milford Square

Morrisville

New Britain

New Hope

Newtown

Perkasie

Penns Park

Pineville

Pipersville

Plumsteadville

Point Pleasant

Quakertown

Richboro

Riegelsville

Rushland

Sellersville

Silverdale

Solebury

Southampton

Springtown

Telford

Trevose

Trumbauersville

Tullytown

Warminster

Warrington

Washington Crossing

Wrightstown

Yardley

# Andalusia

Mathias Antiques
863 Bristol Pike
Andalusia, PA
(215) 639-5111

# Bensalem

Old Mill Flea Market
Water St.
Bensalem, PA
(215) 757-1777

# Blooming Glen

Myers Antiques
712 Blooming Glen Rd.
Blooming Glen, PA
(215) 257-7615

Roger S. Wright Furniture LTD
911 S. Perkasie Rd.
Blooming Glen, PA
(215) 257-5700
(Reproduction & custom furniture.)

# Bristol

Another Time Antiques
307 Mill St.
Bristol, PA
(215) 788-3131

The Place
5 Pond Rd.
Bristol, PA
(215) 785-1494

C & C Auction
2801 Crest Avenue
Bristol, PA
(215) 785-4305

# Buckingham

Bianco Gallery
3921 Rt. 202
Buckingham, PA
(215) 348-4235
(Old & new art)

Rice's
6326 Greenhill Rd.
Buckingham, PA
(215) 297-5993
(Flea markets only, every Tues & Sat.
6:30 am)

Brown Brothers Auction Gallery
Rt. 413
Buckingham, PA
(215) 794-7630
(Auctions every Saturday.)

Robertson & Thornton
4092 Rt. 202
Buckingham, PA
(215) 794-3109

Edna's Antique Shop
General Greene Inn
Rt. 263 & Rt. 413
Buckingham, PA
(215) 794-7261

## Carversville

Brick Cellar Country Antiques
Stover's Mill Rd.
Carversville, PA
(215) 297-5845

Duomo Antiques
3350 Aquaetong Rd.
Carversville, PA
(215) 297-5500
(By appointment only.)

## Chalfont

Bucks County Emporium
8 Skyline Dr.
Chalfont, PA
(215) 997-3227
(56 dealers)

Robillard Auctioneers & Appraisers
8 Skyline Dr.
Chalfont, PA
(215) 997-6887
(Call for auction dates & times.)

Guthrie & Larason Antiques
2 East Butler Ave. (Rt. 202)
Chalfont, PA
(215) 822-3987

## Cornwells Heights

James G. Ambler, Jr.
1221 Sunset Lane
Cornwells Heights, PA
(215) 638-1315

Viola Nicholas
848 Roberts Rd.
Cornwells Heights, PA
(215) 639-2377

## Doylestown

Arieta Ltd.
3175 Burnt House Hill Rd.
Doylestown, PA
(215) 794-8721

Nejad Gallery Fine Oriental Rugs
Main & State Sts.
Doylestown, PA
(215) 348-1255

Best of France at Chestnut Grove
Rt. 202
Doylestown, PA
(215) 345-4253

Renaissance Furnishings
635 N. Main St.
Doylestown, PA
(215) 348-3455

C.R. Notoris Antique Clocks
11 W. Court St.
Doylestown, PA
(215) 230-7180

The Frog Pond
70 W. State St.
Doylestown, PA
(215) 348-3425

Doylestown Antique Center
Rt. 313
Doylestown, PA
(215) 345-9277
(Over 10 dealers.)

The Orchard Hill Collection
4445 Lois Lane
Doylestown, PA
(215) 230-7771

Dragon's Den of Antiques
135 S. Main St.
Doylestown, PA
(215) 345-8666

Three Bridges
5025 Landisville Road
Doylestown, PA
(215) 348-2821 / (800) 562-5968

Edison Furniture Store
1880 Easton Rd.
Doylestown, PA
(215) 348-5841

# Dublin

Emele's Antiques
443 Rt. 313
Dublin, PA
(215) 249-9123

Grandmother's House
Routes 313 & 113
Dublin, PA
(215) 249-0808

Hodge Podge Antiques
232 Rt. 313
(Between Doylestown & Quakertown)
Dublin, PA
(215) 249-9482

Kramer's Rainbow Rooms
104 Middle Rd.
Dublin, PA
(215) 249-1916

The Country Gift Shop
Rt. 313
Dublin, PA
(215) 249-9877
(Reproductions)

# Feasterville

Ruth Cariola Antiques
335 E. Myrtle Ave.
Feasterville, PA
(215) 322-7360
(By appointment.)

# Forest Grove

Tomlinson's Antiques
1823 Forest Grove Rd.
Forest Grove, PA
(215) 794-2991

# Fountainville

Ridge Farm Antiques
Rt. 313 (Part of the Ann Bailey Complex)
Fountainville, PA
(215) 348-1321

# Furlong

Artefact
790 Edison Furlong Rd. & Rt. 263
Furlong, PA
(215) 794-8790

Cash Cow-Folksmith
790 Edison Furlong Rd.
Furlong, PA
(215) 794-2118

Country Collage
Edison Furlong Rd. & Rt. 263
Furlong, PA
(215) 794-3772

# Gardenville

Durham Cabinet Shop
Rt. 413
Gardenville, PA
(215) 766-7104

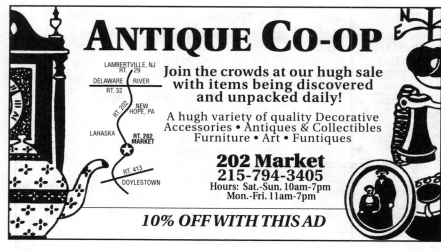
### Holicong

202 Market
Rt. 202
Holicong, PA
(215) 794-3405

Key & Quill Shop
5246 York Rd.
Holicong, PA
(215) 794-3321
(Reproductions & Custom Furniture)

### Hulmeville

Another Man's Treasures
13 Trenton Rd. (Trenton & Main Sts.)
Hulmeville, PA
(215) 702-7210

Old Mill Flea Market
Trenton & Hulmeville Rds.
Hulmeville, PA
(215) 757-1777

Miller Topia Designers
518 Washington Ave.
Hulmeville, PA
(215) 757-3004

### Ivyland

Susan Golashovsky
180 Jacksonville Rd.
Ivyland, PA
(215) 441-8060

The Cat & The Penguin, Ltd.
363 Almshouse Rd. (Rt. 332)
Ivyland, PA
(215) 357-7879

### Lahaska

Alba Limited
5979 Rt. 202
Lahaska, PA
(215) 794-8228

Ariel's
Penn's Market
Rt. 202
Lahaska, PA
(215) 794-5276

Antique Addicts Attic
Rt. 202
Lahaska, PA
(215) 794-2152
(10 dealers)

Auntie Q's
Rt. 202
Lahaska, PA
(215) 794-5410

148

# Lahaska (continued)

Charlie's Girl Tin Shop
1448 Street Rd.
Lahaska, PA
(215) 794-8974
(Historically correct reproduction
  lighting.)

Cottage Farms Antiques
Rt. 202
Lahaska, PA
(215) 794-0840

Darby-Barrett Antiques
Rt. 202
Lahaska, PA
(215) 794-8277

Grady's Antiques
6123 Rt. 202
Lahaska, PA
(215) 794-5532

Joan Kramer Antiques
5788 Rt. 202
Lahaska, PA
(215) 794-8734

Knobs 'n Knockers
Peddler's Village
Lahaska, PA
(215) 794-8045

Lahaska Antique Courte
Rt. 202
Lahaska, PA
(215) 794-7884
(12 dealers)

Maria'a Antiques
Rt. 202
Lahaska, PA
(215) 794-3452

Oaklawn Metalcraft & Antiques
Rt. 202
Lahaska, PA
(215) 794-7387
(Lighting & tools)

Past Time Accents of Yesteryear
Peddler's Village
Lahaska, PA
(215) 794-8499
(Reproductions)

Pickets Post
5761 Rt. 202
Lahaska, PA
(215) 794-7350

Something Old Something New Ltd.
5860 York Rd.
Lahaska, PA
(215) 794-3778/(609) 582-7618

Union Drummer Boy
5820 Rt. 202
Lahaska, PA
(215) 794-8975

## Langhorne

Cottage Crafters
Langhorne Square Shopping Center
Rt. 1
Langhorne, PA
(610) 366-9222

## Levittown

J & M Collectables
6923 Bristol Pike (Rt. 13)
Levittown, PA
(215) 547-2544

Nana's Attic
1037 Oxford Valley Rd.
Levittown, PA
(215) 946-7746

# Lumberville

Reading Antiques
3715 River Rd.
Lumberville, PA
(215) 297-9970

# Mechanicsville

Hamilton Hyre's Buck House
    Antiques
3336 Durham Rd. (Rt. 413)
Mechanicsville, PA
(215) 794-8054

Howard Szmolko Antiques & Fine
    American Furniture
5728 Mechanicsville Rd.
Mechanicsville, PA
(215) 794-8115

# Milford Square

Milford Antiques & Used Furniture
Route 663 on Milford Square Pike
Milford Square, PA
(215) 536-9115

Pieces of Time
Route 663 & Allentown Rd.
Milford Square, PA
(215) 536-3135

# Morrisville

Carousel Consignment Shop
833 W. Trenton Ave.
Morrisville, PA
(215) 295-2461

Richard's Flower Market
305 W. Trenton Ave.
Morrisville, PA
(215) 736-2320

# New Britain

Consignment Galleries
470 Clemens Towne Center (Rt.202)
New Britain, PA
(215) 348-5244

Y-Know Shop
New Galena Rd. & Rt. 313
New Britain, PA
(215) 249-9120

Frank J. Udinson
134 Iron Hill Rd.
New Britain, PA
(215) 345-1725

# New Hope

A'brial's Antiques & Collectibles
Rt. 202 (Across from winery)
New Hope, PA
(215) 794-2887/(610) 828-5669

Cherubim
401 W. Bridge St.
New Hope, PA
(215) 862-2622

Antiquities Museum Shop
86 S. Main St.
New Hope, PA
(215) 862-5002
(Museum reproductions)

Christopher House
31 W. Mechanic St.
New Hope, PA
(215) 862-2722

Clock Trader
6106 Lower York Rd. (Rt. 202)
New Hope, PA
(215) 794-3163

Bridge Street Old Books
129 W. Bridge St.
New Hope, PA
(215) 862-0615

Cockamamie's
9A Bridge St.
New Hope, PA
(215) 862-5454

Crown & Eagle Antiques Inc.
Route 202
New Hope, PA
(215) 794-7972

David Mancuso
Rt. 202 & Upper Mountain Rd.
New Hope, PA
(215) 794-5009

Don Robert's Antiques
38 W. Ferry St.
New Hope, PA
(215) 862-2702

Ferry Hill
15 W. Ferry St.
New Hope, PA
(215) 862-5335

Francis J Purcell II
88 N. Main St.
New Hope, PA
(215) 862-9100

Gardner's Antiques
Rt. 202
New Hope, PA
(215) 794-8616/794-7759

Grady's Antique Furniture
Rt. 202
New Hope, PA
(215) 794-5532

Grandmother's Flower Garden
10 Randolph St. (East)
New Hope, PA
(215) 862-0955

Hall & Winter
429 York Rd.
New Hope, PA
(215) 862-0831

Hobensack & Keller
57 Bridge St.
New Hope, PA
(215) 862-2406

Ingham Springs Antique Center
Rt. 202
New Hope, PA
(215) 862-2145

Katy Kane Antiques Inc.
34 W. Ferry St.
New Hope, PA
(215) 862-5873

Kennedy Antiques
6154 Lower York Rd.
New Hope, PA
(215) 794-8840

Merndale Antiques
429 York Rd. (Rt.202)
New Hope, PA
(215 862-2886

Old Hope Antiques
Rt. 202
New Hope, PA
(215) 862-5055

Oriental Gallery
6444 Rt. 202
New Hope, PA
(215) 862-0366

Pastime Antiques
19 N. Main
New Hope, PA
(215) 862-2366

Queripel Interiors
93 W. Bridge St.
New Hope, PA
(215) 862-5830
(By Appointment)

Raymond James & Co.
6319 Lower York Rd. (Rt. 202)
New Hope, PA
(215) 862-9751

Robert H. Yaroschuk
11 Fishers Alley
New Hope, PA
(215) 862-3912

# New Hope (continued)

Ronley at Limeport
2780 River Rd.
New Hope, PA
(215) 862-2427

Sally Goodman's Frivolite
21 West Ferry St.
New Hope, PA
(215) 862-5754
(Open weekends or by appointment.)

The Black Manx
39 W. Ferry St.
New Hope, PA
(215) 862-3747

The Pink House Antiques
Bridge St. (Rt. 179)
New Hope, PA
(215) 862-5947

Trappings
6444 Lower York Rd.
New Hope, PA
(215) 862-0981

Windy Bush Gallery
3569 Windy Bush Road
New Hope, PA
(215) 862-0714
(art)

## Newtown

Antiques
106 N. State St.
Newtown, PA
(215) 968-2640/295-4989

Hanging Lamp Antiques
140 N. State St.
Newtown, PA
(215) 968-2015

Legacy Gallery
151 N. State St.
Newtown, PA
(215) 579-4421

Miller & Company
15 S. State St.
Newtown, PA
(215) 968-8880

Newtown Antiques
231 N. State St.
Newtown, PA
(215) 968-6475

Temora Farm Antiques
372 Swamp Rd.
Newtown, PA
(215) 860-2742

## Perkasie

Christian Hubscher
100-H W. Callowhill St.
Perkasie, PA
(215) 257-3001

Phillip R. High
1200 Branch Rd.
Perkasie, PA
(215) 257-5714

Treasure Trove
6 S. 7 St.
Perkasie, PA
(215) 257-3564

## Penns Park

Red Sleigh Antiques
2310 Second Pike (Rt. 232)
Penns Park, PA
(215) 598-3017

# Pineville

Midge's Barn Antiques
740 Rt. 413
Pineville, PA
(215) 598-3304

Pineville Antiques
1084 Durham Rd.
Pineville, PA
(215) 598-8795

# Pipersville

Nadia's Trash or Treasure
Easton Rd. (Rt. 611)
10 miles North of Doylestown
Pipersville, PA
(215) 766-7827

# Plumsteadville

Tess Sands Connections & Antiques
5912 Rte. 611
Plumsteadville, PA
(215) 766-9593

Heckler's Antiques
Rt. 611
Plumsteadville, PA
(215) 766-0532

# Point Pleasant

1807 House
4962 River Rd. (Rt. 322)
Point Pleasant, PA
(215) 297-0599

River Run Antiques
166 River Rd.( Rt. 32)
Point Pleasant, PA
(215) 297-5303

Furniture Mill
Tollgate & Swagger Rds.
Point Pleasant, PA
(215) 297-8505

Rosebud Antiques
6183 Carversville Rd.
Point Pleasant, PA
(215) 297-5109

Jacques M. Cornillion
56 Byram Rd.
Point Pleasant, PA
(215) 297-5854

# Quakertown

Curio Corner
E. Broad St. & Hellerstown Ave.
(Intersection of Rts. 212 & 313)
Quakertown, PA
(215) 536-4547

Grandpa's Treasures
137 E. Broad St.
Quakertown, PA
(215) 536-5066

Dunngeon Antiques & Interiors
215 W. Broad St.
Quakertown, PA
(215) 538-9355

J P &Kids
2335 Hillcrest Rd.
Quakertown, PA
(215) 536-5566

Pat & Lou's Curiosity Shop
513 N. Westend Blvd.
Quakertown, PA
(215) 536-8248

Flying Tiger Antiques
2305 Mill Hill Rd.
Quakertown, NJ
(215) 536-1042

Quaker Antique Mall
701 Tollgate Rd.
Quakertown, PA
(215) 538-9445
(100 dealers)

Quakertown Heirlooms
141 E. Broad St. & Hellertown Rd.
(Corner of Rts. 313 & 212)
Quakertown, PA
(215) 536-9088

The Flying Frog
132 E. Broad St.
Quakertown, PA
(215) 536-5630

Trolley House Emporium
108-114 E. Broad St.
Quakertown, PA
(215) 538-7733

## Richboro

Lyons Antiques
86 E. Windrose Dr.
Richboro, PA
(215) 396-4750
(By appointment only.)

## Riegelsville

Allen's Antiques
666 Easton Rd. (Rt. 611)
Riegelsville, PA
(610) 749-0337

Rivertown Gallery
1126 Easton Rd. (Rt. 611)
Riegelsville, PA
(610) 749-0944

## Rushland

Old Maps & Prints
987 Penns Park Rd.
Rushland, PA
(215) 598-3662
(By appointment only.)

## Sellersville

Bittersweet Shoppe
202 N. Main St.
Sellersville, PA
(215) 257-0944

Buck's Trading Post
930 Old Bethlehem Pike
Sellersville, PA
(215) 453-0323/453-0623

## Silverdale

Gehman School House Antiques
Rt. 113 & Telegraph Rd.
Silverdale, PA
(215) 257-7196

## Solebury

Lehmann Antiques
6154 Lower York Rd. (Rt. 202)
Solebury, PA
(215) 794-7724

Whitley Studio
Laurel Rd.
Solebury, PA
(215) 297-8452

# Southampton

Auctions by Stephenson's
1005 Industrial Blvd.
Southampton, PA
(215) 322-6182
(Auctions every Friday at 3:00.)

# Springtown

Long Spring Antiques
2789 Slifer Valley Rd. & Hickory Lane
Springtown, PA
(610) 346-7659
(American Indian artifacts, jewery & weaponry, by appointment only)

# Telford

Byron Hecker Cabinetmaker
260 Telford Pike
Telford, PA
(215) 721-1566

Telford Exchange
527-B South Main St.
Telford, PA
(215) 723-9870

Koffel's Curiosity Shop
26 Madison Ave.
Telford, PA
(215) 723-9365

# Trevose

The Brownsville Antique Centre
1918 Brownsville Rd.
Trevose, PA
(215) 364-8846

# Trumbauersville

James A. Meyers Antiques
330 Broad St.
Trumbauersville, PA
(215) 538-0723
(By appointment only.)

Trumbauersville Antiques
19 E. Broad St.
Trumbauersville, PA
(215) 536-6305

# Tullytown

Wilhemina's Antiques
369 Main St.
Tullytown, PA
(215) 945-8606

# Warminster

Interior Consignment Galleries
Davisville Shopping Center
Street Rd & Davisville Rd.
Warminster, PA
(215) 396-8000
(used furniture)

Scarpill's Antiques
857 Mearns Rd. (1/2 mile North of
   Street Rd.)
Warminster, PA
(215) 675-4303
(By appointment only.)

# Warrington

First Penn Precious Metals, Inc. &
    G & G Antiques
25 N. Easton Road (Rt. 611)
Warrington, PA
(215) 674-5910

Upstairs Downstairs Interiors
215 Pebble Ridge Rd.
Warrington, PA
(215) 343-6605

# Washington Crossing

Dynasty Antiques
1113 General Washington Memorial
    Blvd.
Washington Crossing, PA
(215) 493-6941

Hanging Lamp Antiques
1077 River Rd.
Washington Crossing, PA
(215) 493-0563

Forager House
968 Taylorville Rd.
Washington Crossing, PA
(215) 493-3007

# Wrightstown

Bucks County Art & Antiques Co.
532 Durham Rd. (Rt. 413)
Wrightstown, PA
(215) 345-1885

Trading Post Antiques
532 Durham Rd. (Rt. 413)
Wrightstown, PA
(215) 579-1020

Nostalgia Nook
591 Durham Rd. (Rt. 413)
Carousel Village
Wrightstown, PA
(215) 598-8837

# Yardley

Antiques in Yardley
70 S. Main St.
Yardley, PA
(215) 493-0137

Carolyn Jeannes Antiques
747 Stoney Hill Rd.
Yardley, PA
(215) 493-6294

C. L. Prickett
930 Stoney Hill Rd. (Just off I-95 &
    Rt.332)
Yardley, PA
(215) 493-4284

# Chester County

Atglen
Avondale
Berwyn
Birchrunville
Chadds Ford
Chester Springs
Coatesville
Cochranville
Devon
Downingtown
Eagle
Exton
Frazer
Guthriesville
Kemblesville
Kennett Square
Kimberton
Knauertown
Lionville
Malvern
Marshallton
Mendenhall
New London
Oxford
Paoli
Parkesburg
Phoenixville
Spring City
Strafford
Thorndale
Toughkenamon
Unionville
Valley Forge
West Chester
West Grove

# Atglen

Family Country Crafts
Gap Village Store
Atglen, PA
(717) 442-5263

Penns Farm Antiques
107 Zook Rd.
Atglen, PA
(610) 593-1776

# Avondale

Antiques & Images At Avondale
Box 902 Gap-Newport Pike
Avondale, PA
(610) 268-0226
(7 dealers)

Kaolin 1770 Shoppe
316 Sunny Dell Rd.
Avondale, PA
(610) 268-2592/268-2816

# Berwyn

...And Antiques
19 Waterloo Ave.
Berwyn, PA
(610) 644-3659

McCoy Antiques & Interiors
722 W. Lancaster Ave.
Berwyn, PA
(610) 640-0433

Anything & Everything Shop
36 Waterloo Ave.
Berwyn, PA
(610) 647-8186

Pennsylvania Art Conservatory
636 Lancaster Ave.
Berwyn, PA
(610) 644-4300
(18th century art)

Circa Antiques & Decor
712 Lancaster Ave.
Berwyn, PA
(610) 651-8151

Surrey Consignment Shop
16 Waterloo Rd.
Berwyn, PA
(610) 647-8632

Deja vu Antiques
11 Waterloo Rd.
Berwyn, PA
(610) 296-2737

Eldred Wheeler
15 Waterloo Ave.
Berwyn, PA
(610) 640-0470
(Fine 18th cent. reproduction
   furniture.)

# Birchrunville

Richard Wright Antiques
Hollow & Flowing Springs Rds.
Birchrunville, PA
(610) 827-7442

## Chadds Ford

Aaron Goebel's Antiques
261 South Rt. 202
Chadds Ford, PA
(610) 459-8555

Antique Reflections
Village Shoppes at Chadds Ford
170 Fairville Rd.
Chadds Ford, PA
(610) 388-0645

Barbara & Co, Inc. Ltd.
516 Kennett Pike
Village of Fairville
Chadds Ford, PA
(610) 388-8445

Brandywine River Antiques Market
878 Baltimore Pike
Chadds Ford, PA
(610) 388-2000

Brandywine Exchange
Rt. 202
Chadds Ford, PA
(610) 558-2020

Candlelight Antiques & Collectibles
1110 Smithbridge Rd.
Chadds Ford, PA
(610) 358-6053

Cantona & Milbourn Antiques
Barn Bldg. (next to Chadds Ford Inn)
Rts. 1 and 100
Chadds Ford, PA
(610) 388-8680

Diane's Antiques
Rt. 1
Chadds Ford, PA
(610) 388-3956

Elizabeth L. Matlat
134 Wilmington Pike/Rt. 202
Brandywine Summit Center
Glen Millls, PA
(610) 358-0359

Frances Lantz Country Antiques
Rt. 202 & State Line Rd.
Chadds Ford, PA
(610) 459-4080

French Country Antiques
708 Oakbourne Rd.
Concordville/Chadds Ford
(610) 692-0445

John F. Joyce
1611 Baltimore Pike
Chadds Ford, PA
(610) 388-7075

Olde Ridge Village Antique Shops
Rt. 202 & Ridge Rd.
Chadds Ford, PA
(610) 459-0960

Paul Maynard Antiques
536 Kennett Pike (Rt. 53)
Village of Fairville
Chadds Ford, PA
(610) 388-6521

Pennsbury-Chadds Ford Antique Mall
Rt. 1
Chadds Ford, PA
(610) 388-6546/388-1620

Pitt's Antiques
95 Baltimore Pike
Chadds Ford, PA
(610) 558-8950/(302) 475-0894

Rogers H. Hopkins
Old Baltimore Pike
Chadds Ford, PA
(610) 388-7160

Spring House
101 Baltimore Pike
Chadds Ford, PA
(610) 388-7075

Stockard's Attic
Rt. 1 & Rt. 100
Chadds Ford, PA
(610) 388-9588

The Village Peddlar
161B-Baltimore Pike
Chadds Ford, PA
(610) 388-2828

The Wooden Knob
Rt. 1 & 100
Chadds Ford, PA
(610) 388-3861

Wendy's Corner
210 Wilmington Pike (Rt. 202)
Chadds Ford, PA
(610) 358-4077

## Chester Springs

Centuries Ltd. Antiques
At the Rising Sun Tavern
1251 Conestoga Rd.
Chester Springs, PA
(610) 827-3054

Chester Springs Antiques
1733 Conestoga Rd.
Chester Springs, PA
(610) 827-2229

Gatherings
Shops at Pickering Mill
Rt. 113 & Yellow Springs Rd.
Chester Springs, PA
(610) 827-1870

## Coatesville

Chet Ramsay Antiques
2460 Strasburg Rd.
Coatesville, PA
(610) 384-0514

Donald Howe Antiques
360 Harmony St.
Coatesville, PA
(610) 384-3615

Windle's Log Cabin Antiques
Gum Tree Rd.
Coatesville, PA

## Cochranville

Cottonwood Exchange
Corner of Rts. 10 and 41
Cochranville, PA
(610) 593-7995/(800) 982-9666

## Devon

Joseph & Peter Antiques
Devon Design Center
111 E. Lancaster Ave.
Devon, PA
(610) 254-0600

Old Forest Antiques
34 N. Waterloo Rd.
Devon, PA
(610) 989-1700

## Downingtown

Collector's Corner
31 E. Lancaster Ave.
Downingtown, PA
(610) 269-9196

Downingtown Farmers Market
Rt. 30
Downingtown, PA
(610) 518-5100
(Open Fri., Sat. & Sun., 10+ indoor
    dealers. Outdoor flea market in
    good weather.)

Frantiques
527 W. Lancaster Ave.
Downingtown, PA
(610) 269-4307

Gary Pennington
5031 Horseshoe Pike (Rt. 322)
Downingtown, PA
(610) 873-6966

Oak Emporium Antiques
147 E. Lancaster Ave.
Downingtown, PA
(610) 269-3632

Philip H. Bradley Co.
1101 East Lancaster Ave.
(E. Lincoln Hwy. )
Downingtown, PA
(610) 269-0427

Pook & Pook, Inc.
113 & Bus. Rt. 30
Downingtown, PA
(610) 269-4040
(Showroom by appointment. Call for
    auction times)

Smith Auction Co.
Downingtown, PA
(610) 269-1036
(Call for auction dates, times &
    Locations)

Swoyers Fine Art & Collectibles
116 E. Lancaster Ave.
Downingtown, PA
(610) 269-3838

# Eagle

Eagle Emporium
100 & Byers Rd.
Eagle, PA
(610) 458-7188

Little Bit Of Country
Rt. 100
Eagle, PA
(610) 458-0363

The Eagle Lantern
Rt. 100
Eagle, PA
(610) 458-8964
(18th cent. reproduction lighting)

# Exton

Ball & Ball
436 W. Lincoln Hwy.
Exton, PA
(610) 363-7330
(Original & antique hardware,
    lighting, furniture & fireplace
    equipment.)

John W. Bunker & Son
431 E. Lincoln Hwy.
(Business Rt. 30)
Exton, PA
(610) 363-7436

Jonathan Schill Antiques
609 W. Lincoln Hwy.
Exton, PA
(610) 594-6200

My Best Junk
Rt. 100
Exton, PA
(610) 524-1116

William McCarraher Appraisals &
    Auction Services
609 W. Lincoln Hwy. (Business Rt. 30)
Exton, PA
(610) 363-0341

# Frazer

Antiquities
Lincoln Court Shopping Center
Rt. 30
Frazer, PA
(610) 408-8898

Folk Furnishings
178 W. Lancaster Ave.
Frazer, PA
(610) 695-8686

Frazer Antiques
351 Lancaster Ave.
Frazer, PA
(610) 651-8299

Stevens Antiques
627 Lancaster Ave.
Frazer, PA
(610) 644-8282

# Guthriesville

Hodge Podge Shoppe
Rt. 322 Horseshoe Pike
Guthriesville, PA
(610) 269-7735

# Kemblesville

Harold S. Hill & Son Inc.
Rt. 896
Kemblesville, PA
(610) 274-8525
(Auctions every other Sat.)

# Kennett Square

Antiquus
120 W. State St.
Kennett Square, PA
(610) 444-9892

Clifton Mill Shoppes
162 Olde Kennett Rd.
Kennett Square, PA
(610) 444-5234

Fancy Branches Florist & Antiques
104 W. State St.
Kennett Square, PA
(610) 444-5063

Longwood Garrett
864 E. Baltimore Pike (Rt. 1)
Kennett Square, PA
(610) 444-5257

McLimans
940 W. Cypress St.
Kennett Square, PA
(610) 444-3876

Perennials Thrift Shop
19 New Garden Town Square
350 Scarlett Rd.
Kennett Square, PA
(610) 444-1438

Period Furniture Designs
Rt. 926 & Rt. 82
Kennett Square, PA
(610) 444-6780
(Reproductions)

The Moon Dial
101 E. Locust Lane
(Off Rt. 82N.)
Kennett Square, PA
(610) 444-2995

Thomas Macaluso Used & Rare Books
130 S. Union St. (Rt. 82)
Kennett Square, PA
(610) 444-1063

# Kimberton

Corner Cupboard Antiques, Inc.
Kimberton Rd.
Kimberton, PA
(610) 933-9700

Kimber Hall
Hares Hill Rd.
Kimberton, PA
(610) 933-8100

Thorums
Prizer Rd.
Kimberton, PA
(610) 933-3121
(Open every Thurs & Fri. and on the
first and last Sat. of every month.)

# Knauertown

H. D. Wilder
Rt. 23
Knauertown, PA
(610) 469-9774

# Lionville

The Hawley House
95 E. Welsh Pool Rd.
Lionville, PA
(610) 594-9790

# Malvern

Antique Galleria
The Shoppes at Nob Hill
288 Lancaster Ave.
Malvern, PA
(610) 644-7996

Capriola's Architectural Antique &
   Salvage
Warren Ave.
Malvern, PA
(610) 647-3380
(Open Saturday or by appointment.)

Conestoga Antiques
Conestoga Rd.
Malvern, PA
(610) 647-6627

Hobby Horse
Sugartown Rd.
Malvern, PA
(610) 644-2386
(Furniture crafted from antique wood
   salvage.)

Kendall Chew & John Formicola
690 Sugartown Rd.
Malvern, PA
(610) 647-3339

King Street Fine Art & Antiques
148 E. King St.
Malvern, PA
(610) 251-9949

King Street Traders
16 E. King St.
Malvern, PA
(610) 296-8818

**Nesting Feathers
218 E. King St.
Malvern, PA
(610) 408-9377
(31 Dealers and Gourmet Cafe)**

Portobello Road
138 E. King St.
Malvern, PA
(610) 647-7690

Station House Antiques Ltd.
1 W. King St.
Malvern, PA
(610) 647-5193

The Cranberry Cellar
148 E. King St.
Malvern, PA
(610) 647-7763

The Olde General Store
2447 Yellow Springs Rd.
Malvern, PA
(610) 647-8968/644-1734

Van Tassel & Baumann/
   The Collector's Assistant
690 Sugartown Rd.
At the Sharpless-Worrall House in
   Historic Sugartown
Malvern, PA
(610) 647-3339

# Marshallton

The Blacksmith Shop
1340 W. Strasburg Rd. (Rt. 162)
Marshallton, PA
(610) 696-2469

# Mendenhall

Antique Reflections
170 Fairville, Rd.
Mendenhall, PA
(610) 388-0645

William Hutchinson
330 Kennett Pike (Rt. 52)
Mendenhall, PA
(610) 388-0195/388-2010
(Books, prints & art)

J & L West Antiques
Rt. 52 & Fairville Rd.
Mendenhall, PA
(610) 388-2014

Sally Borton Antiques
Kenntt Pike (Rt. 52)
Village of Fairville
Mendenhall, PA
(610) 388-7687

# New London

Jack In The Pulpit Gift Shoppe
Rt. 896 & State Rd.
New London, PA
(610) 869-4144

# Oxford

Antiques at Ramsgate
Lower Hopewell Rd.
Oxford, PA
(610) 932-5052

Phillips Sale Barn
204 Limestone Rd.
Oxford, PA
(610) 932-5858

Marketplace Preowned Furniture
405 Market St.
Oxford, PA
(610) 932-4110

Shank's Barn
12700 Limestone Rd.
Oxford, PA
(610) 932-9212

Nottingham Used Furniture
11152 Baltimore Pike
Oxford, PA
(610) 932-4397

The Muxim Room
Old Rt. 1 (Rt. 10 through town)
Oxford, PA
(610) 932-2993

# Parkesburg

Cackleberry Farm Antique Mall
5003 Rt. 30
Parkesburg, PA
(717) 442-8805

Olde Town Treasures
Olde Main St
Parkesburg, PA
(610) 857-2649

Parkesburg Country Store
221 Olde Main St.
Parkesburg, PA
(610) 857-1252

Pheasant Run Antiques
4824 W. Lincoln Hwy.
Parkesburg, PA
(717) 442-4090

The Paxson House
4201 West Lincoln Highway
Parkesburg, PA
(610) 857-5750

# Paoli

King of Prussia Antiques
538 Foxwood Lane
Paoli, PA
(610) 251-9299

Richard Herzog Upholstery
44 North Valley Rd.
Paoli, PA
(610) 695-9770
(18th & 19th cent. Reproduction
    furniture)

The Paoli Meadows
Chestnut Village Shoppes
Paoli, PA
(610) 889-9202

# Phoenixville

A Different World Antiques
238 Bridge St.
Phoenixville, PA
(610) 983-9881

Another Time Collectibles
320 Bridge St.
Phoenixville, PA
(610) 935-8860/(215) 483-5262

Bridge Street Fine Arts & Antiques
234 Bridge Street
Phoenixville, PA
(610) 917-9898

Eye of the Phoenix
222 Bridge St.
Phoenixville, PA
(610) 917-8444

Kari's Korner
Corner Whitehorse Rd & Valley Forge
    Rd. (Rt. 23)
Phoenixville, PA
(610) 935-1251

Kathleen Rais & Co.
847 Valley Forge Rd.
Phoenixville, PA
(610) 935-1251

Martin Dale
234 Bridge St.
Phoenixville, PA
(610) 917-9898

Old Picket Fence
The Shop of Korner Stores
843-847 Valley Forge Rd.
Phoenixville, PA
(610) 917-9992

## Phoenixville (continued)

Oohs & Ahs
245 Bridge St.
Phoenixville, PA
(610) 917-8271

Peter Scioli Used Furniture
235 Bridge Street
Phoenixville, PA
(610) 935-0118

Phoenixville Antiques
237 Bridge St.
Phoenixville, PA
(610) 933-8477

The Copper Rooster
847 Valley Forge Rd. (Rt. 23)
Phoenixville, PA
(610) 917-9965

Somogyl Antiques
129 Rt. 113
Phoenixville, PA
(610) 933-5717

The Shop Around The Corner
26 S. Main St.
Phoenixville, PA
(610) 983-4477

Tomes of Glory
The Shop of Korner Shops
843-847 Valley Forge Rd.
Phoenixville, PA
(610) 935-9510

## Spring City

Rich Moyer's Bonnie Brae Auction Co.
2 Bonnie Brae Rd.
Spring City, PA
(610) 948-8050
(Auctions held every other Saturday,
    3:00pm.)

Samuel G. Hultz Antiques
820 Pughtown Rd.
Spring City, PA
(610) 469-9491

## Strafford

Gordon S. Converse and Co.
Spread Eagle Village
Strafford, PA
(610) 964-7632

Interiors
Spread Eagle Village
503 W. Lancaster Ave.
Strafford, PA
(610) 989-9665

Wilson's Main Line Antiques
329 E. Conestoga Rd.
Strafford, PA
(610) 687-5500

## Thorndale

Eric Chandlee Wilson
16 Bondsville Rd, (Rt. 340)
Thorndale, PA
(610) 383-5597
(clocks)

## Toughkenamon

New Garden Stable Shops
New Garden Rd.
Toughkenamon, PA
(610) 268-0428
(12 Shops)

## Unionville

Crystal Spring Farm Antiques
Rt. 842 & Mill Rd.
Unionville, PA
(610) 347-0380

The Merry-Go-Round Room
Rt. 82
Unionville, PA
(610) 347-0482

## Valley Forge

Mullen Antiques
Rt. 23 & Pawlings Rd.
Valley Forge, PA
(610) 933-2324

---

# R.M. WORTH ANTIQUES
## ——————INC.——————
### 18th & 19th Century American Furniture, Painting and related Decorative Arts.

1388 Old Wilmington Pike, West Chester, PA 19382
610-399-1780  Fax: 610-399-1978

Hours: Monday by appointment, Tuesday-Saturday 10am-6pm, Sunday 12pm-5pm

---

## West Chester

Ann Powers Antiques & Brass Beds
1497 Wilmington Pike
West Chester, PA
(610) 459-4662

Baldwin's Book Barn
865 Lenape Rd.
West Chester, PA
(610) 696-0816

Bring and Buy Shop
E. Gay St. & Gay St. Plaza
West Chester, PA
(610) 696-2576

County Seat Antiques & Furnishings
41 W. Gay St.
N.E. Corner of Church & Gay Sts.
West Chester, PA
(610) 696-0584

Darrel's Antiques
Brinton's Bridge Rd. & Rt. 202
West Chester, PA
(610) 399-0536
(Open weekends or by apptointment.)

David K. Ely Antiques
20 Ellis Lane
West Chester, PA
(610) 696-4593

Dilworthtown Country Store
275 Brintons Bridge Rd.
West Chester, PA
(610) 399-0560
(Reproductions)

Flightstone Antiques
1029 Shiloh Road
West Chester, PA
(610) 399-0795

H. L. Chalfant
1352 Paoli Pike
West Chester, PA
(610) 696-1862

Herbert Schiffer Antiques
1469 Morstein Rd.
West Chester, PA
(610) 696-1521

Herman Woolfrey Antiques
1433 S. Whitford Rd.
West Chester, PA
(610) 363-2073
(By appointment)

J. Palma Antiques
1144 Old Wilmington Pike
West Chester, PA
(610) 399-1210

John F. Weeks
743 W. Miner St.
West Chester, PA
(610) 696-7327

Monroe Coldren Antiques
723 E. Virginia Ave.
West Chester, PA
(610) 692-5651

Newsome, Thomas & Morris Antiques
106 W. Market St.
West Chester, PA
(610) 344-0657

O'Brien's Art & Antiques
Market St. & Darlington
West Chester, PA
(610) 918-9855

Old Mill Antiques
20 N. Ellis La.
West Chester, PA
(610) 696-4593

Olivier Fleury, Inc.
708 Oakborne Rd.
West Chester, PA
(610) 692-0445

Partner's Used Furniture
125 W. Market St.
West Chester, PA
(610) 431-6639

Penwick-The Hayloft
132 N. High St.
West Chester, PA
(610 431-2739

Polito Antiques
820 Sconneltown Rd.
West Chester, PA
(610) 696-4860

Rose Valley Restorations
132 East Prescott Alley
West Chester, PA 19380
(610) 738-8323

RM Worth Antiques Inc.
1388 Old Wilmington Pike
West Chester, PA
(610) 399-1780/ 388-2121

Spring Meadows Farm Antiiques.
Dorset Dr.
West Chester, PA
(610) 793-3616
(By appointment)

The Antique Shop
106 W. Market St.
West Chester, PA
(610) 344-0657

## West Chester (continued)

William H. Bunch Gallery
11 N. Brandywine St.
West Chester, PA
(610) 696-1530
(Auctions every other Tuesday, 4:00.)

Women's Exchange
10 S. Church St.
West Chester, PA
(610) 696-3058

## West Grove

Barbara Hood's Country Store
378 Hoods Lane
West Grove, PA
(610) 869-8437

West Grove Resale Shop
306 E. Baltimore Pike
West Grove, PA
(610) 869-9950

# Delaware County

Aston
Booths Corner
Chester Heights
Collingdale
Concordville
Drexel Hill
Fernwood
Glen Mills
Glenolden
Gradyville
Havertown
Holmes
Lansdowne
Media
Newtown Square
Prospect Park
Ridley Park
Sharon Hill
Swarthmore
Upland
Upper Darby
Villanova
Wayne
Woodlyn

# Aston

Martins Auction
142 Rt. 322
Aston, PA
(610) 497-7745
(Auctions every other Tuesday.)

# Booths Corner

Robert BriggsAuction
1315 Naamans Creek Rd.
Booths Corner, PA
(610) 566-3138/485-0412
(Auctions held Friday & Saturday.)

R.L. Beck
1104 Naamans Creek Rd.
Booths Corner, PA
(610) 459-3476
(Reproduction furniture)

Booth's Corner Farmers Market
1362 Naaman's Creek Rd.
Booths Corner, PA
(610) 485-0775

# Chester Heights

Wilson's
342-344 Valleybrook Rd.
Chester Heights, PA
(610) 565-1616
(Call for auction dates & times.)

# Collingdale

Tony Liberato Coins & Stamps
920 MacDade Blvd.
Collingdale, PA
(610) 534-2404

# Concordville

Heirloom Restorations & Antiques
990 Baltimore Pike (Rt. 1)
Concordville, PA
(610) 459-3380

# Drexel Hill

Ardmart Antique Village
State Rd & Lansdowne Ave.
Drexel Hill, PA
(610) 789-6622
(40 dealers)

Clock Services
2255 Garrett Rd.
Drexel Hill, PA
(610) 284-2600

Fields Antique Jewelers
Lansdowne & Windsor Aves.
Drexel Hill, PA
(610) 853-2740

Springhouse Antiques
4213 Woodland Ave.
Drexel Hill, PA
(610) 623-8898

# Fernwood

Scavanger's Haven
19 Church Lane
Fernwood, PA
(610) 626-7442

# Glen Mills

Candlelight Antiques
1110 Smithbridge Rd.
Glen Mills, PA
(610) 358-6053

Pratt & Company
128 Glen Mills Rd.
Glen Mills, PA
(610) 558-3404
(Antiques & Reproductions)

# Glenolden

Uniques & Antiques
204 N. Chester Pike
Glenolden, PA
(610) 583-2000/521-9473
(Call for auction dates & times.)

# Gradyville

Den of Antiquity
Rt. 352 & Gradyville Rd.
Gradyville, PA
(610) 459-2209/459-2836

Gradyville Services Inc.
Rt. 352 (Middletown Rd.) &
    Gradyville Rd.
Gradyville, PA
(610) 459-2208

# Havertown

Tamerlane Books
516 Kathmere Rd.
Havertown, PA
(610) 449-4400

# Holmes

Rita's Relics
215 Holmes Rd.
Holmes, PA
(610) 534-7070

# Lansdowne

Ann's Antiques
213 W. Baltimore Pike
Lansdowne, PA
(610) 623-3179

Good Old Days Antiques
201 E. Plumstead Ave.
Lansdowne, PA
(610) 622-2688

Before Our Times Antiques
54 W. Marshall Rd.
Lansdowne, PA
(610) 259-6370

Lansdowne Auction Galleries
11 S. Lansdowne Ave.
Lansdowne, PA
(610) 622-6836/622-6936
(Auctions every Tuesday)

# Lansdowne (continued)

P & J Antiques & Collectables
609 Baltimore Ave.
Lansdowne, PA
(610) 626-2010

Ye Olde Thrift Shoppe
213 W. Baltimore Ave.
Lansdowne, PA
(610) 623-3179

Robert C. James Furniture Specialist
141 E. Plumstead Ave.
Lansdowne, PA
(610) 259-6699
(Small selection of items, primarily
   refinishing.)

## Media

Antique Exchange of Media
23 W. State St.
Media, PA
(610) 891-9992

Rhodes Affordable Place
200 W. Baltimore Pike
Media, PA
(610) 566-4436

Atelier
36 W. State St.
Media , PA
(610) 566-6909

The Fitzgerald Group
220 W. Baltimore Ave.
Media, PA
(610) 566-0703

Remember When
21 W. State St.
Media, PA
(610) 566-7411

## Newtown Square

The Consign & Design Gallery
3716 West Chester Pike
Newtown Square, PA
(610) 359-8889

Tymes Remembered Antiques
15 Alban's Circle
Newtown Square, PA
(610) 353-9677

## Prospect Park

Dom Di Placido Antiques
1040 Lincoln Ave.
Prospect Park, PA
(610) 583-5525

Tri State Antiques
1100 Lincoln Ave.
Prospect Park, PA
(610) 237-0746

## Ridley Park

The Barn Auction House
440 Chester Pike
Ridley Park, PA
(610) 521-9473
(Auctions held every Friday at 6:00.)

## Sharon Hill

Audrey's Used Furniture
421 Sharon Ave.
Sharon Hill, PA
(610) 461-6274

## Swarthmore

Cricket Way LTD
102 Park Ave
Swarthmore, PA
(610) 604-0225

Swarthmore Antiques Ltd.
343 Dartmouth Ave.
Swarthmore, PA
(610) 874-8601

## Upland

Serendipity Shop - CCMC
One Medical Center Blvd.
Upland, PA
(610) 872-2428

## Upper Darby

Delaware Valley Thrift & Antiques
809 Garrrett Road
Upper Darby, PA
(610) 352-9430

Park Avenue Shop
26 Park Ave. & S. Cedar Lane
Upper Darby, PA
(610) 446-4699

Henry A. Gerlach
414 S. State Rd.
Upper Darby, PA
(610) 449-7600
(clocks, jewelry & art)

## Villanova

Elinor Gordon
Villanova, PA
(610) 525-0981
(Chinese export porcelain. By appt. only.)

## Wayne

Consignment Galleries
163 W. Lancaster Ave.
Wayne, PA
(610) 687-2959

Hunt Auctions Inc./The Pembroke
   Shop
167 W. Lancaster Ave.
Wayne, PA
(610) 688-8185

Knightsbridge Antiques Ltd.
121 N. Wayne Ave.
Wayne, PA
(610) 971-9551

Lifestyle Treasures
405 W. Wayne Ave.
Wayne, PA
(610) 688-5909
(Open Saturday, 10:00-12:00 or by
   appointment.)

Neighborhood League Shop
191 Lancaster Ave.
Wayne, PA
(610) 687-5758

Painted Past
201 E. Lancaster Ave.
Wayne, PA
(610) 293-7420
(Handmade & custom furniture from
architectural & construction salvage.)

Scallywag Antiques
308 W. Lancaster Ave.
Wayne, PA
(610) 688-8212

The Antique Collection
161 Lancaster Ave.
Wayne, PA
(610) 902-0600

The Old Store
238 Lancaster Ave.
Wayne, PA
(610) 688-3344

## Woodlyn

B & W Collector's Shop
1937 W. MacDade Blvd.
Woodlyn, PA
(610) 872-1042

# Lancaster County

Adamstown
Bart
Brickerville
Bird In Hand
Blue Ball
Christiana
Columbia
Denver
Drumore
Ephrata
Gap
Holtwood
Kinzers
Lancaster
Leola
Lititz
Little Britain
Manheim
Marietta
Middletown
Millersville
Mount Joy
Myerstown
Neffsville
New Holland
Paradise
Quarryville
Reamstown
Ronks
Reinholds
Schaefferstown
Soudersburg
Strasburg
Willow Street

## Adamstown

Adamstown Antique Mall
Rt. 272
Adamstown, PA
(717) 484-0464

Alternative Furnishings
Rt. 222
1 mi. North of Adamstown
(610) 796-2990

Antiques Showcase at the Blackhorse
2222 N. Reading Rd. PA turnpike Exit
    21 & Rt. 272 N.
Denver, PA
(717) 335-3300
(300 dealers)

Apple Works Antique Mall
Rt.272
Adamstown, PA
(717) 484-4404

Clock Tower Antiques
Behind the Stoudtburg\Black Angus
Adamstown, PA
(717) 484-2757

Exit 21 Antiques
Rt. 272
Adamstown, PA
(717) 484-1300

General Heath's Antiques
Rt. 272 & Calico Rd.
Adamstown, PA
(717) 484-1300

Greenwood Antique Center
2455 North Reading Rd.
Adamstown, PA
(717) 335-3377

Heritage I Antique Center
Rt. 272
Adamstown, PA
(717) 484-4646
(65 dealers)

Heritage II Antique Center
Rt. 272
Adamstown, PA
(717) 336-0888
(40 dealers)

Meade Antiques
Rt. 272
Adamstown, PA
(717) 484-0669

Olde Smith Farm
Rt. 272
Adamstown, PA
(717) 484-2611

Oley Valley Architectural Antiques
Rt. 272
Adamstown, PA
(717) 335-3585

Renningers Antique Market
Rt. 272
Adamstown, PA
(717) 336-2177

Shupp's Grove
Rt. 897
Adamstown, PA
(717) 484-4115
(Outdoors only)

South Pointe Antiques
Rt. 272 & Denver Rd.
Adamstown, PA
(717) 484-1026

Stoudtburg/ Black Angus Antiques
    Mall
Rt. 272
Adamstown, PA
(717) 484-4385
(over 500 dealers)

Tex Johnson Antiques
40 Willow St.
Adamstown, PA
(717) 484-4005

The Country French Collection
Rt. 272
Adamstown, PA
(717) 484-0200

The Ladies Shop
Rt. 272
Adamstown, PA
(717) 484-1219

## Bart

Oak Furniture & Antiques
Rt. 896
Bart, PA
(717) 786-7852

## Brickerville

The 1857 Barn Antiques
Corner Rts. 501 & 322
Brickerville, PA
(717) 626-5115

Brickerville Antiques & Decoys
117 E. Division St. (Rt. 322)
Brickerville, PA
(717) 627-2464

Nailor Antiques
Rt. 322
Brickerville, PA
(717) 626-9508

Rice Antiques
Rt. 322 (1/4 mile east of Rt. 501)
Brickerville, PA
(717) 627-3780
(By appointment only.)

## Bird In Hand

Farmhouse Antiques
519 Beechdale Rd.
Bird In Hand, PA
(717) 656-4854

Helen G. Warren
6878 Old Philadelphia Pike
Bird In Hand, PA
(717) 392-4233

## Blue Ball

Carson's Country Stew
Rt. 322 & Grist Mill Rd.
Blue Ball, PA
(717) 354-7343

# Christiana

Irion Company Furnituremakers
1 S. Bridge St.
Christiana, PA
(610) 593-2153
(18th cent. furniture made to order.)

# Columbia

Angela House Antiques
401 Chesnut St.
Columbia, PA
(717) 684-4111

Partners Antique Center
403 N. Third St.
Columbia, PA
(717) 684-5364

C.A. Herr Antiques & Collecibles
  Co-op
25-29 North 3rd St.
Columbia, PA
(717) 684-7850

Restorations Etc.
125 Bank Ave.
Columbia, PA
(717) 684-5454

Nora's Antiques & Gifts
Corner of Second & Locust Sts.
Columbia, PA
(717) 684-8864

# Denver

Adams Antiques
2400 N. Reading Rd. (Rt. 272)
Denver, PA
(717) 335-0001

Denver Fine Arts Gallery
Reading Rd. (Rt. 272)
Denver, PA
(717) 484-4811
(Fine art, open Sunday or by
  appointment.)

Adamstown Antique Gallery
Rt. 272 (South)
Denver, PA
(717) 335-3435

Lancaster County Antique Center
2255 N. Reading Rd. (Rt. 272)
Denver, PA
(717) 336-2701
(70 dealers)

Barr's Auction & Antique World
2152 N Reading Rd. (Rt. 272)
Denver, PA
(717) 336-2861

Covered Bridge Antiques &
  Collectibles
Rt. 272
Denver, PA
(717) 336-4480
(40 dealers)

# Drumore

Jockey Lot Antiques & Flea Marker
1130 Lancaster Pike
Drumore, PA
(717) 284-4984/284-4965

# Ephrata

Antiques at Ephrata
1749 W. Main St.
Ephrata, PA
(717) 738-4818
(5 dealers)

Good's Collectibles
246 W. Main St.
Ephrata/Clay, PA
(717) 788-2033

Grandma's Attic
1862 W. Main St.
Ephrata, PA
(717) 733-7158

Mother Tucker's Antiques
566 N. Reading Rd.
Ephrata, PA
(717) 738-1297

Olde Carriage House Shop
2425 W. Main St.
Ephrata, PA
(717) 733-1111

South Pointe Antiques
Rt. 272 & Denver Rd.
Ephrata, PA
(717) 484-1026

Summerhouse Antiques
1156 W. Main St.
Ephrata, PA
(717) 733-6572/733-8989
(By appointment only.)

Three T's Antiques
Rt. 322 West
Ephrata, PA
(717) 733-6572

# Gap

Don & Ann's Antique Row
5297 Lincoln Hwy. East
Gap, PA
(717) 442-3026

N & N Sales
835 Rt. 41
Gap, PA
(717) 442-4668

Rich Man, Poor Man
Rt. 30 (East)
(Next to Brass Eagle restaurant)
Gap, PA
NO Phone

# Holtwood

Rocky Hill Stripping & Refinishing
Susquehannock Dr.
Holtwood, PA
(717) 284-3376

# Kinzers

The Way We Were Antiques
5015 E. Lincoln Hwy.
Kinzers, PA
(717) 442-0978

# Lancaster

American Period Lighting
3004 Columbia Ave.
Lancaster, PA
(717) 392-5649
(Traditional & period lighting)

Antiques & Uniques
1545 Oregon Pike
Lancaster, PA
(717) 397-9119

Beechtree Antiques
1249 Penn Grant Rd.
Lancaster, PA
(717) 687-6881

Carlos' Antiques
339 W. Orange St.
Lancaster, PA
(717) 299-0785

Estate Liquidations
1001 Lititz Ave.
Lancaster, PA
(717) 399-8156

Fleckenstein's Gifts
738 Columbia Ave.
Lancaster, PA
(717) 397-2585

Levi H. Hersey
2194 Old Philadelphia Pike
Lancaster, PA
(717) 397-5794

Moongate Antiques
27 Prince St.
Lancaster, PA
(717) 393-9910

Olde Towne Interiors, Inc.
224 W. Orange St.
Lancaster, PA
(717) 394-6482

Pandora's Antiques
2014 Old Philadelphia Pike
Lancaster, PA
(717) 299-5305

Robert H. Linton
147 Bender Mill Rd.
Lancaster, PA
(717) 872-4331
(handcrafted reproductions)

The Book Haven
146 N. Prince St.
Lancaster, PA
(717) 393-0920

The Buy & Sell Store
107 W. King St.
Lancaster, PA
(717) 397-5542

The Finishing Touch
801 N Shippen St.
Lancaster, PA
(717) 397-0511

Violet's Antiques
Hager Archade Building
Lancaster, PA
(717) 293-5710

Willcox Gallery
117 E. Chestnut St.
Lancaster, PA
(717) 295-5414

Zap & Company
320 N. Queen St.
Lancaster, PA
(717) 397-7405

# Leola

Antiques & Uniques
110 W. Main St.
Leola, PA
(717) 656-6950

Meadowbrook Farmers Market
W. Main St.
Leola, PA
(717) 656-2226

# Lititz

E.M. Murry Associates
23 N. Water St.
Lititz, PA
(717) 626-2636
(Call for auction dates & time.s)

Garthoeffner Gallery Antiques
122 E. Main St.
Lititz, PA
(717) 627-7998

H.B. Hardican Antiques
34 E. Main St.
Lititz, PA
(717) 627-4603

Heritage Map Museum
55 N. Water St.
Lititz, PA
(717) 626-5002

Sue's Back Porch
6 Zum Anker Alley
Lititz, PA
(717) 625-2110

Sylvan Brandt
653 Main St.
Lititz, PA
(717) 626-4520
(18 & 19th cent. building materials)

The Workshop
945 Disston View Rd.
Lititz, PA
(717) 626-6031

# Little Britain

Joy's Antiques
400 Nottingham Rd. (Rt. 272)
Little Britain, PA
(717) 529-2693

# Manheim

Conestoga Auction Company Inc.
768 Graystone Rd.
Manheim, PA
(717) 898-7284
(Call for auction dates & times.)

Exit 20 Antiques
3091 Lebanon Road (Rt. 72 N.)
Exit 20 on PA Trnpk.
Manheim, PA
(717) 665-5008

Gerald E. Noll
1047 S. Colebrook Road
Manheim, PA
(717) 898-8677

Manheim Country Store Antiques &
   Museum
60 N. Main St.
Manheim, PA
(717) 664-0022

Stone Barn Antiques
Chiquies Road
Manheim, PA
(717) 898-1895

# Marietta

Marietta Mobil Antiques &
   Collectibles
271 W. Market St.
Marietta, PA
(717) 426-2390

Perry House
30 E State St.
Marietta, PA
(717) 426-4560

# Middletown

Days Gone By
Intersection Geyers Church Rd. & Rt. 442
Middletown, PA
(717) 944-4934

# Millersville

Birk's Antiques & Things
20 Sun Lane
Millersville, PA
(717) 872-4706/872-8959

# Mount Joy

Angelina's Antique Shop
1195 W. Main St.
Mt. Joy, PA
(717) 653-0505

White Horses Antiques Market
973 W. Main St (Rt. 230)
Mount Joy, PA
(717) 653-6338
(125 dealers)

# Myerstown

Union Canal Antique Mall
Rt. 422 (West)
Myerstown, PA
(717) 866-7635

# Neffsville

Dorothy Forster Antiques
2778 Lititz Pike (Rt. 501)
Neffsville, PA
(717) 354-9153

Richard Hilton
2650 Lititz Pike
Neffsville, PA
(717) 569-6901

# New Holland

School House Farm Antiques
Rt. 322
New Holland, PA
(717) 354-9153

# Paradise

Brackbill's Country Antiques
3187 Lincoln Hwy. E. (Rt. 30)
Paradise, PA
(717) 687-6719

JP Collectibles & Flea Market
Rt. 30 E.
Paradise, PA
(717) 442-8892

H & H Auctions\Micklemine's
   Auction
1904 Mine Rd.
Paradise, PA
(610) 593-5550
(Call for auction dates & times)

Lichty's Clock Shop
10 Cherry Hill Rd.
Paradise, PA
(717) 687-9243

## Paradise (continued)

Mary & Eds Upholstery & Antique
   Shop
Rt. 30
Paradise, PA
(717) 687-8990

Paradise Village Antiques
3044 Lincoln Hwy. (East)
Paradise, PA
(717) 687-8089
(20 dealers)

Spring Hollow Antiques
121 Mt. Pleasant Rd.
Paradise, PA
(717) 687-6171

## Quarryville

Erma's Flower Shop & Antiques
State St.
Quarryville, PA
(717) 786-2512

Jayne's Antiques & Collectibles
27 E. State St.
Quarryville, PA
(717) 786-8028

## Reamstown

The Doll Express, Inc.
Rt. 272
Reamstown, PA
(717) 336-2414

## Ronks

Antique Barn
Rt. 30
Ronks, PA
(717) 687-7088

Country Antiques
2855 Lincoln Hwy.
Ronks, PA
(717) 687-7088

Dutch Barn Antiques
3272 W. Newport Rd.
Ronks, PA
(717) 768-3067

JA-Bar Enterprises
2812 Lincoln Hwy.
Ronks, PA
(717) 393-0098

The Antique Market Place
2856 Lincoln Hwy. (Rt. 30)
East Ronks, PA
(717) 687-6345

## Reinholds

Oley Valley Country Store
2684 N. Reading Rd.
Reinholds, PA
(717) 484-2191

## Schaefferstown

Antiques on the Square
Main & Market Sts.
Schaefferstown, PA
(717) 949-2819(717) 687-6345

## Soudersburg

The Antique Marketplace
2856 Lincoln Hwy.
Soudersburg, PA
(717) 687-6345

## Strasburg

Frey's Antiques
209 W. Main St.
Strasburg, PA
(717) 687-6722

Iron Star Antiques
53 W. Main St.
Strasburg, PA
(717) 687-8027
(By appointment)

Miller's Country Collectibles
215 Hartman Bridge Rd.
Strasburg, PA
(717) 687-0490

MR 3L's Antiques & Collector Center
2931 Lincoln Hwy. (Rt..30)
Strasburg, PA
(717) 687-6165

Spring Hollow Antiques
121 Mt. Pleasant Rd.
Near Strasburg
(717) 687-6171

Strasburg Antique Market
At Rts. 896 & 741
Strasburg, PA
(717) 687-5624
(60+ dealers)

Sugarbush Antiques
832 May Post Office Road
Strasburg, PA
(717) 687-7179

William Wood & Son Old Mill
  Emporium
215 Georgetown Rd.
Strasburg, PA
(717) 687-6978

## Willow Street

Aichele's Refinishing
366 Baumgardner Road
Willow Street, PA
(717) 464-5244

Tomorrow's Treasures
Willow Street, PA
(717) 394-4987
(By appointment)

# Lehigh County

Allentown
Bethlehem
Coopersburg
Emmaus
Fogelsville
Fullerton
Macungie
New Tripoli
Slatington
Whitehall
Zionsville

# Allentown

Affordable Antiques
15381/2 Gordon St.
Allentown, PA
800-457-1335/(610)770-9990

Abe Ark Antiques
S. Cedar Crest Blvd.
Allentown, PA
(610) 770-1454
(By appointment only.)

Another Story
100 N. 9th St.
Allentown, PA
(610) 435-4433

B & B Antiques & Collectables
12 N. 7th St. (Corner Hamilton & 7th)
Allentown, PA
(610) 820-9588

Burick's Antiques
880 N. Graham St.
Allentown, PA
(610) 432-8966

Camelot Gallery
1518 Walnut St.
Allentown, PA
(610) 433-7744

Cottage Crafters Craft & Antique Mall
Tighlman Shopping Center
4636 Broadway St.
Allentown, PA
(610) 366-9222

Duvall's Antiques & Nice Collectibles
43 N. 9th St.
Allentown, PA
(610) 821-4878
(By appointment only.)

Estate Sales Inc.
Hamilton Blvd. & Minesite Rd.
Allentown, PA
(610) 366-8337

Golden Eagle Antiques
1425 Gordon St.
Allentown, PA
(610) 432-1223
(By appointment only.)

K D Smith Auctions
S. 12th & Vultee St.
Allentown, PA
(610) 797-1770
(Auctions held every Sunday at 12:00.)

Lehigh Valley Antiques
415 N 15th St.
Allentown, PA
(610) 439-1117
(Open Sat. & Sun. only.)

Little House Antiques
2705 S. Old Pike Ave.
Allentown, PA
(610) 791-2802

Lutz & Moyer
936 Allen St.
Allentown, PA
(610) 820-9924

Merchants Square Mall
S. 12th & Vultee St.
Allentown, PA
(610) 797-7743
(Over 40 shops.)

Pete's Used Furniture & Antiques
231 N. 7th St.
Allentown, PA
(610) 433-4481
(Call before visiting)

Toonerville Junction Antiques
522 Maple St.
Allentown, PA
(610) 435-8697

# Bethlehem

Appleton's
2825 Cross Creek Rd.
Bethlehem, PA
(610) 866-9838

C & D Coin & Gun
125 E. Broad St.
Bethlehem, PA
(610) 865-4355

In The Olde Manner
7 E. Church St.
Bethlehem, PA
(610) 974-9247

Opportunities Knocks Twice
Third Street
Bethlehem, PA
(610) 866-8663

R & R Collectibles
224 Nazareth Pike
Bethlehem, PA
(610) 759-5610

Splendid Choices
Rt. 378 & Walter Ave.
Bethlehem, PA
(610) 691-8311

Valley Antiques, Gifts & Imports
729 W. Broad St.
Bethlehem, PA
(610) 865-3880

Wadsworth & Co.
107 E. Third St.
Bethlehem, PA
(610) 866-1577

William Howard-Flea Market
East Third St.
Bethlehem, PA
(610) 317-8330

Yesterday' Ltd.
2311 Center St.
Bethlehem, PA
(610) 691-8889
(By appointment only.)

# Coopersburg

Liberty Metal Finishing Company
113 John Alley
Coopersburg, PA
(610) 282-1719
(Antique brass & copper items)

# Emmaus

Lawsons Antiques & Collectibles
5386 Chestnut St.
Emmaus, PA
(610) 966-4375

Twin Jugs
4033 Chestnut St.
Emmaus, PA
(610) 967-4010

# Fogelsville

Fogelsville Auction Center
Nursery St.
Fogelsville, PA
(610) 395-9643
(Auctions held every Thurs, 2:00 PM)

Ralph Zettlemoyer Auction Co.
815 Nursery St.
Fogelsville, PA
(610) 395-8084
(Auctions every Thursday)

# Fullerton

Old Dairy Antique Village
105 Franklin St.
Fullerton, PA
(610) 264-7626

# Macungie

Lacey's Treasures
165 E. Main St. (Rt. 100)
Macungie, PA
(610) 966-5177

# New Tripoli

W. S. Phillips
4555 Golden Key Rd.
New Tripoli, PA
(610) 285-6290

# Slatington

Charlotte's Web Country Store
1044 Main St.
Slatington, PA
(610) 760-8787

Watrings Auction Center
3320 Church St. (Rt. 873)
Slatington, PA
(610) 767-8610
(Call for auction dates & times.)

D. L . Stevens Antiques
560 Main St.
Slatington, PA
(610) 760-0685

Lutz Moyer Antiques
200 Willow Ave.
Slatington, PA
(610) 760-1919

# Whitehall

Nejad Gallery Fine Oriental Rugs
2350 MacArthur Rd.
Whitehall, PA
(610) 776-0660

Old Dairy Antiques
105 Franklin St.
Whitehall, PA
(610) 264-7626

# Zionsville

Zionsville Antique & Craft Mall
7567 Chestnut St.
Zionsville, PA
(610) 965-3292
(150 dealers)

# Montgomery County

Abington
Ambler
Ardmore
Bala Cynwyd
Blue Bell
Bryn Mawr
Collegeville
Colmar
Conshohocken
Creamery
Eagleville
East Greenville
Elroy
Flourtown
Fort Washington
Gilbertsville
Gladwyne
Glenside
Green Lane
Harleysville
Hartford
Hatboro
Haverford
Hatfield
Huntingdon Valley
Jeffersonville

Jenkintown
King of Prussia
Kulpsville
Lafayette Hill
Lansdale
Lederach
Montgomeryville
Narberth
Norristown
North Wales
Palm
Pennlyn
Pennsburg
Plymouth Meeting
Pottstown
Roslyn
Royersford
Schwenksville
Skippack
Souderton
Sumneytown
Worcester
Wynnewood
Zieglersville

# Abington

Abington Antique Shop
1165 Old York Rd.
Abington, PA
(215) 884-3204

# Ambler

John J. Mcfadden
1 E. Butler Ave.
Ambler, PA
(215) 540-8866

Ross G. Gerhart
55 N. Main St.
Ambler, PA
(215) 646-0474

The Antique Drummer
216 Lindenwold Ave.
Ambler, PA
(215) 628-9535
(By appointment only)

# Ardmore

Amalia F. Milione
2713 Haverford Rd.
Ardmore, PA
(610) 896-5770
(By appointment only.)

Ardmore Antiques and Oriental Rugs
321 W. Lancaster Ave.
Ardmore, PA
(610) 649-4432

Daniel Wilson
24 E. Lancaster Ave.
Ardmore, PA
(610) 645-9533

En Garde Antiques & Collectibles
2-4 Lancaster Ave.
Ardmore, PA
(610) 645-5785

Golf-Tiques & Collectibles
8 Anderson Ave.
Ardmore, PA
(610) 642-6171/(609) 344-3826
(By appointment only.)

Harry's Treasures and Collectibles
317 W. Lancaster Ave.
Ardmore, PA
(610) 642-4775

Interior Works
28 Rittenhouse Place
Ardmore, PA
(610) 658-0155
(Antique accessories)

Porter's Book Store
24 Ardmore Ave.
Ardmore, PA
(610) 896-8913

# Bala Cynwyd

General Eclectic
195 Bala Ave.
Bala Cynwyd, PA
(610) 667-6677

Pieces of Tyme
323 Montgomery Ave.
Bala Cynwyd, PA
(610) 664-2050

# Blue Bell

Troll House Antiques
910 Valley Rd.
Blue Bell, PA
(215) 646-3166/800-470-4842

# Bryn Mawr

American Ordinance Preservation
  Association Inc.
311 Millbank Rd.
Bryn Mawr, PA
(610) 519-9610
(Military antiques, by appointment
  only.)

Bryn Mawr Hospital Thrift Shop
County Line Rd. (Behind the hospital)
Bryn Mawr,PA
(610) 526-9533/525-5488

Bryn Mawr Mini Antique Mart
844 County Line Rd.
Bryn Mawr, PA
(610) 525-8922

Greentree Gallery
825 W. Lancaster Ave.
Bryn Mawr, PA
(610) 526-1841

Main Line Consignments
706 E. Lancaster Ave.
Bryn Mawr, PA
(610) 526-2837

Sandy De Maio
860 W. Lancaster Ave.
Bryn Mawr, PA
(610) 525-1717

Susan Vitale Antiques
835 W. Lancaster Ave.
Bryn Mawr, PA
(610) 527-5653

# Collegeville

Abbott Antiques
1700 Main St.
Collegeville, PA
(610) 489-0667

Back Door Shoppes
466 Main St.
Collegeville, PA
(610) 489-6520

Quail Nest
315 E. Main St.
Collegeville, PA
(610) 454-9368

The Bejamin Cox House Herbary
310 Black Rock Rd.
In the Village of Oaks
Collegeville, PA
(610) 933-5036

The Power House
45 1st Ave. (Off 29)
Collegeville, PA
(610) 489-7388
(Open Sunday only.)

Trappe Antiques & Restoration
1639 W. Main St. (Rt. 422 Business)
Collegeville-Trappe, PA
(610) 489-0714

# Colmar

Barbie J's Antiques
842 Bethlehem Pike
Colmar, PA
(215) 822-7624

# Conshohocken

The Outbound Station
2 Harry St.
Conshohocken, PA
(610) 825-3825

Nelly's Place
14 E 5th Ave.
Conshohocken, PA
(610) 825-7971

# Creamery

Jerry's Antiques & Used Furniture
Rt. 113
Creamery, PA
(610) 409-9479

# Eagleville

Bountiful Antiques
Colonial Shopping Ctr.
Eagleville, PA
(610) 539-0210

# East Greenville

Fuddy Duddy Antiques &
  Memorabilia
239 Main St.
East Greenville, PA
(215) 541-4449

Nanna's Nook & Cranny/
  Paulette Krick
239 Main Street Plaza
East Greenville, PA
(215) 679-8686

# Elroy

The Drafty Barn
117 Allentown Rd.
Elroy, PA
(215) 721-1677

# Flourtown

Bob's Antiques & Used Furniture
1505 Bethlehem Pike
Flourtown, PA
(215) 233-9007

The Treasure Hunter
1614 Bethlehem Pike
Flourtown, PA
(215) 233-4026

Frank Griffith Antiques
1520 Bethlehem Pike
Flourtown, PA
(800) 929-2226

# Fort Washington

Dolores & Irvin Boyd Antiques
509 Bethlehem Pike
Fort Washington, PA
(215) 646-5126

Michael J. Whitman Antiques
427 Bethlehem Pike
Fort Washington, PA
(215) 646-8639
(By appointment)

Meetinghouse Antiques
509 N. Bethelehm Pike
Fort Washington, PA
(215) 646-5126

The Green Tureen Antique Shop
431 Bethlehem Pike
Fort Washington, PA
(215) 628-3792

# Gilbertsville

Shafer's Antiques
1573 E. Philadelphia Ave.
Gilbertsville, PA
(610) 367-5630

# Gladwyne

Schwarz Gallery
815 Black Rock Rd.
Gladwyne, PA
(610) 642-1500

# Glenside

Infield Sport Collectibles
276 Keswick Ave.
Glenside, PA
(215) 947-2625

Pinky Lil' Hammer
235 Keswick Ave.
Glenside, PA
(215) 884-6722

Kirland & Kirkland
237 Keswick Ave.
Glenside, PA
(215) 576-7771

Sadie's Early Birds
16 E. Glenside Ave.
Glenside, PA
(215) 572-1116

Ludwig's Scattered Treasures
221 W. Glenside Avenue
Glenside, PA
(215) 887-0512

Yesterday & Today
280 Keswick Ave.
Glenside, PA
(215) 572-6926

# Green Lane

Colonial House Antiques
Corner Routes 29 & 63
Green Lane, PA
(215) 234-4113
(By appointment)

Seneca Arms Company, Inc.
116 Gravel Pike
Green Lane, PA
(215) 234-8984
(Civil War firearms)

# Harleysville

Old Mill Antiques of Harleysville
279 Maple Ave.
Harleysville, PA
(215) 256-9957

# Hartford

Phil's Used Furniture & Antiques
Routes 29 & 100
Hartford, PA
(215) 679-8625

# Hatboro

Joys & Toys
53 S. York Rd.
Hatboro, PA
(215) 675-2880

Treasures From The Past
5 Williams Lane
Hatboro, PA
(215) 672-3511

Steven Fosbrook Jr. Antiques
134 S. York Rd.
Hatboro, PA
(215) 674-0704

# Hatfield

Alderfer Auction Co.
501 Fairgrounds Rd.
Hatfield, PA
(215) 393-3000
(Auctions every Thursday.)

# Haverford

Antiques Upstairs
17A Haverford Station Rd.
Haverford, PA
(610) 896-0624

James S. Jaffe Rare Books
367 W. Lancaster Ave
Haverford, PA
(610) 649-4221

Chelsea House Ltd
45 Haverford Station Rd.
Haverford, PA
(610) 896-5554

McClees Galleries
343 W. Lancaster Ave.
Haverford, PA
(610) 642-1661

French Corner Antiques
16 Haverford Station Rd.
Haverford, PA
(610 ) 642-6867

The Mock Fox
15 Haverford Station Rd.
Haverford, PA
(610) 642-4990

# Huntingdon Valley

Noreen's Antiques
1700 Huntingdon Pike
Huntingdon Valley, PA
(215) 947-9890

Valley Antiques & Collectibles LTD
2531 Huntingdon Pike (2nd St. Pike)
Huntingdon Valley, PA
(215) 947-7858

# Jeffersonville

Stephen Arena Antiques
2118 W. Main St.
Jeffersonville, PA
(610) 631-9100

# Jenkintown

Anthony's Curiosity Shop
805 Greenwood Ave.
Jenkintown, PA
(215) 885-2992

Breslin Consignment Corner
719 West Ave.
Jenkintown, PA
(215) 884-5444

# Jenkintown (continued)

Hidden Treasure
425 Leedom St.
Jenkintown, PA
(215) 887-7305

Jeffrey Ceasar Antiques
214 Old York Rd.
Jenkintown, PA
(215) 572-6040

Jenkintown Antique Guild
208 York Rd.
Jenkintown, PA
(215) 576-5044

Palinurus-Antiquarian Books
101 Greenwood Avenue
Jenkintown, PA
(215) 884-2297
(Books, science, medicine &
 economics, pre-1840)

# King Of Prussia

Weigh Back When Antiques
251 S. Henderson Rd.
King of Prussia, PA
(610) 992-1692

Mon Magasin
502 Henderson Rd.
King of Prussia, PA
(610) 878-9370
(Second hand furniture)

# Kulpsville

Kulpsville Antiques & Flea Market
1375 Forty Foot Rd.
Kulpsville, PA
(215) 361-7910

# Lafayette Hill

The Resettlers Marketplace
651 Germantown Pike
Lafayette Hill, PA
(610) 828-9633/828-9637

# Lansdale

Edwin B. Choyce
7 N. Mitchell St.
Lansdale, PA
(215) 855-3377
(By appointment)

# Lederach

James Galley
816 Cross Rd.
Lederach, PA
(215) 256-9880

# Montgomeryville

The General Hancock Antique Center
735 Bethlehem Pike (corner of Rts. 309 & 463)
Montgomeryville, PA
(215) 361-7404
(45 dealers)

# Narberth

Bruce McKittrick Rare Books Inc.
43 Sabine Ave.
Narberth, PA
(610) 660-0132
(15th to 18th century books, by
    appointment only.)

Robert Tryon
202 Dudley Ave.
Narberth, PA
(610) 617-1055

Ruth Blum Antiques
227 Haverford Ave.
Narberth, PA
(610) 660-8030

# Norristown

Arena'a
Burnside St. & Ridge Pike
Norristown, PA
(610) 631-9100

Auntie Q's
403 W. Marshall St.
Norristown, PA
(610) 279-8002

Daniel Yost Interiors
Dekalb (Rt. 202) & Airy Sts.
Norristown, PA
(610) 272-1000

Debbie's Thrift
522 Marshall St.
Norristown, PA
(610) 272-5005

Felber Ornamental Plastering Corp.
1000 W. Washington St.
Norristown, PA
(610) 275-4713
(period architectural details)

Fryer's Auction
651 W. Germantown Pike & Whitehall
    Rd.
Norristown, PA
(610) 539-1670
(Auctions every Thurs & Sun.)

Larry's Thrift Shop
406 W. Marshall St.
Norristown, PA
(610) 279-6387

Pennsylvania Antiques Marketplace
Logan Square Shopping Center
Rts. 202 & Johnson Hwy.
Norristown, PA
(610) 275-3500
(Open Saturday & Sunday only)

Vij Art & Antiques
1847 Markley St.
Norristown, PA
(610) 275-2026

# North Wales

Sweet Repeats
115 S. Main St.
North Wales, PA
(215) 661-8800

# Palm

The Barnyard at Summer Brook Farm
Rt. 29
Palm, PA
(215) 679-0773

# Penllyn

F.J. Carey III
Penllyn, PA
(215) 643-4664
(By appointment only.)

# Pennsburg

Geryville Country Store
1830 Geryville Pike
Pennsburg, PA
(215) 541-0881

# Plymouth Meeting

Cold Point PA Antiques
2501 Butler Pike
Plymouth Meeting, PA
(610) 825-3342

Plymouth Meeting Gallery
Plymouth Meeting
(610) 825-9068
(Fine art, by appointment only.)

Keith's Antiques Ltd.
Plymouth Meeting Mall
Plymouth Meeting, PA
(610) 828-4933
(Antiques & Reproductions)

# Pottstown

Antiques at Half Crown Farm
1226 Warwick Furnace Rd.
Pottstown, PA
(610) 469-6649/469- 9296

Shaner's Antiques & Collectables
403 N. Charlotte St.
Pottstown, PA
(610) 326-0165

Bill's Carpet Shop
1359 Farmington Ave.
Pottstown, PA
(610) 323-9210
(Selection of antique oriental rugs.)

Thomas R. Galloway
326 N. Charlotte St.
Pottstown, PA
(610) 718-1292

Used To Be
100 W. Schuylkill Rd.
Pottstown, PA
(610) 326-8773

Our Secret Garden
791 S. Hanover St.
Pottstown, PA
(610) 970-1550

# Roslyn

Heirloom Jewel Company
1186 Easton Rd.
Roslyn, PA
(215) 886-3886

# Royersford

Ken Reed Auction Gallery
401 Main St.
Royersford, PA
(610) 948-4871
(Call for auction dates & times.)

# Schwenksville

Need to Be Remembered Antiques & Such
96 Main St.
Schwenksville, PA
(610) 287-7813

# Skippack

Allen Antiques and Artisans
Corner of Valley Forge Rd. & Skippack
  Pike
(Rts. 73 and 363)
Skippack, PA
(610) 584-5559

Douglass' Antiques
3907 Skippack Pike
Skippack, PA
(610) 584-6102

Evergreen Antiques & Things
4036 Skippack Pike
Skippack, PA
(610) 222-0940

From The Past
4039 Skippack Pike
Skippack, PA
(610) 584-5842

Kay's Antiques
3852 Skippack Pike
Skippack, PA
(610) 584-1196

Nostalgia
4034 Skippack Pike (Rt. 73)
Skippack, PA
(610) 584-4112

**Remains to be Seen Antiques**
**4006 Skippack Pike**
**Skippack, PA**
**(610) 584-5770**

Seasons of Skippack
Rt. 73 & Store Rd.
Skippack, PA
(610) 584-6799

Snyder's Antiques
4006 Skippack Pike
Skippack, PA
(610) 584-6454

Thorpe Antiques
4027 Skippack Pike
Skippack, PA
(610) 584-1177

Trout's Antiques & Reproduction
  Furniture
4059 Skippack Pike
Skippack, PA
(610) 584-8466

Upwyth Fine Art Gallery
Corner of Store Rd. & Rt. 73
Skippack, PA
(610) 584-1438

# Souderton

Souderton Antiques
24 Main St.
Souderton, PA
(215) 723-1770

Union Conference Center
24 Main St.
Souderton, PA
(215) 723-1700

Ye Olde Cowpath Antique & Gift
   Shoppe
59 Cowpath Rd. (Rt. 463)
Souderton, PA
(215) 723-5768

# Sumneytown

Sumneytown School House
Sumneytown Pike
Sumneytown, PA
(215) 234-8707

# Worcester

Budroni's Auction Services
1680 Shefley Lane
Worcester, PA
(610) 584-9270

# Wynnewood

Cherchez Ltd. Antiques
Manoa & Haverford Rds.
Wynnewood, PA
(610) 649-1060

# Zieglersville

Chris Scott Antiques
6 Big Rd.
Zieglersville, PA
(610) 287-8266

# Northampton County

**Bath**
**Easton**
**Hellertown**
**Mount Bethel**
**Nazareth**
**Northampton**
**Portland**
**Windgap**

## Bath

Grandma Patty's Antiques
151 N. Chestnut St.
Bath, PA
(610) 837-9633

Steckel House Antiques
Chestnut & Northampton St.
Bath, PA
(610) 837-1660

## Easton

Barry' s New & Used Furniture
500 Northampton St.
Easton, PA
(610) 250-0220

Quadrant Book Mart & Coffee House
20 N. 3rd St.
Easton, PA
(610) 252-1188

Brick House Antiques
1116 Northampton St.
Easton, PA
(610) 515-8010

The Eagle's Nest Antiques
1717 Butler St.
Easton, PA
(610) 258-4092

Dylan Spencer Antiques
200 Northampton St.
Easton, PA
(610) 252-6766

## Hellertown

Achey's Antiques
Hellertown, PA
(610) 838-6212

Buddy K. Toys
24 Durham St.
Hellertown, PA
(610) 838-6505
(By appointment only.)

## Mount Bethel

Chris's Barn Antiques
Rt. 611
Mount Bethel, PA
(610) 599-1064

Family Tree Antiques & Bridal
Rt. 611
Mount Bethel , PA
(717) 897-5683
(By appointment)

## Nazareth

Dotta Auction Co., Inc.
330 W. Moorestown Rd. (Rt. 512)
Nazareth, PA
(610) 433-7555
(Call for auction dates & times.)

Gostony's Auction Center/ The
   Auctioneer Inc.
1035 Bushkill Center Rd.
Nazareth, PA
(610) 759-5674
(Auctions Thurday & Saturday
   evenings.)

Flamisch Antiques & Collectibles
694 Heyer Mill Rd.
Nazareth, PA
(610) 759-6438

## Nazareth (continued)

Nazareth Auction Center
Rt. 512
Nazareth, PA
(610) 759-7389
(Auctions every Wednesday, 2: 00.)

Old Red School House
543 Rose Inn Ave.
Nazareth, PA
(610) 759-6622

Ondris Antiques
534 S. Main St.
Nazareth, PA
(610) 746-0970

## Northampton

Carol Simcoe
2015 Main St.
Northampton, PA
(610) 262-7448

Finders Keepers
Rt. 248
Northampton, PA
(610) 261-2181

Irons Antiques
223 Covered Bridge Rd.
Northampton, PA
(610) 262-9335

Northampton Coin & Jewelry
  Exchange
1918 Center St.
Northampton, PA
(610) 262-0759

## Portland

Graystone Collectiques
511 Delaware Ave. (Rt. 611)
Portland, PA
(717) 897-7170

Kathy's Cove
423 Delaware Ave.
Portland, PA
(717) 897-7223

Knot Necessarily Antiques
425 Delaware Ave.
Portland, PA
(717) 897-5606/897-7140

Indian Joe Curios
Delaware Ave.
Portland, PA
No Phone

Long Ago Antiques
Delaware Ave.
Portland, PA
(717) 897-0407

Portland Antiques & Collectibles
Delaware Ave. (Rt. 611)
Portland, PA
(717) 897-0129

Portland Station
Delaware Ave.
Portland, PA
(717) 897-7695

## Windgap

Browse-A-Bit Shop
1501 Teels Rd.
Windgap, PA
(610) 863-8009

Gerry's Brass & Copper Finishing
464 Albert Rd.
Windgap, PA
(610) 863-9458
(Brass & copper items & refinishing)

# Philadelphia

**Chestnut Hill**
**Manyunk**
**Philadelphia**

# Chestnut Hill

Antiques at the Secret Garden
12-14 East Hartwell Lane
Chestnut Hill, PA
(215) 247-8550

Bird In Hand
8419 Germantown Ave.
Chestnut Hill, PA
(215) 248-2473

Blum's Chestnut Hill Antiques
43-45 East Chestnut Hill Ave.
Chestnut Hill, PA
(215) 242-8877

Chandlee & Bewick
7811 Germantown Ave.
Chestnut Hill, PA
(215 )242-0375

Diane Bryman Orientals
8038 Gernmantown Ave.
Chestnut Hill, PA
(215) 242-4100

Dobbins Oriental Rug Shop
8219 Germantown Ave.
Chestnut Hill, PA
(215) 247-2227

Elaine Cooper
8609 Germantown Ave.
Chestnut Hill, PA
(215) 242-3030

Garden Gate
8139 Germantown Ave.
Chestnut Hill, PA
(215) 248-5190
(20 dealers)

Gilmore's Book Shop
43 E. Chestnut Hill Ave.
Chestnut Hill, PA
(215) 248-1763

Helen L. Jones French Country
   Antiques
8436 Germantown Ave.
Chestnut Hill, PA
(215) 247-4944

Hobe Atelier
7918 Germantown Ave.
Chestnut Hill, PA
215-247-5733
(American art pottery)

McCarty Antiques
7733 Winston Rd.
Chestnut Hill, PA
(215) 247-5220

Porch Cellar Antiques Market
7928-30 Germantown Ave.
Chestnut Hill, PA
(215) 247-1952
(45 dealers)

P.S. Consignment Home Furnishings
8705 Germantown Ave.
Chestnut Hill, PA
(215) 248-3223

Smalls Antiques Market
7932-34 Germantown Ave.
Chestnut Hill, PA
(215) 247-1953

The Antique Gallery
8523 Germantown Ave.
Chestnut Hill, PA
(215) 248-1700

The Leather Bucket
84 Bethlehem Pike
1st fl. Rear
Chestnut Hill, PA
(215) 242-1140

The Philadelphia Print Shop
8441 Germantown Ave.
Chestnut Hill, PA
(215) 242-4750

The Portobello Antiques
Germantown Ave.
Chestnut Hill, PA
(215) 247-0181

The Post Light
51 E. Bethelehem Pike
Chestnut Hill, PA
(215) 242-3810
(18th cent. reproduction lighting)

# MANAYUNK
## ANTIQUE MARKET

# Manyunk

Antique Lighthouse
4400 Dexter St.
Manyunk
Philadelphia, PA
(215) 483-8221
(Restored antique lighting, by
  appointment.)

Antique Marketplace
3797 Main St.
Manyunk
Philadelphia, PA
(215) 482-4499
(Over 100 dealers)

Antique and Not So
100 Leverington Ave.
Manayunk
Philadelphia, PA
(215) 509-7510

Calderwood Gallery
4441 Pechin St.
Manyunk
Philadelphia, PA
(215) 509-6644

Decades Vintage
4369 Cresson St.
Manyunk
Philadelphia, PA
(215) 483-1579/(215) 482-0233
(Vintage Clothing & Textiles)

I Brewster & Co.
Main St.
Manyunk
Philadelphia, PA
(215) 731-9200

Ida's Treasures
4388 Main St. (Corner of Main &
  Levering)
Manyunk
Philadelphia, PA
(215) 482-7060

Manyunk Antique Market & Bond
  Street Gallery
Main & Leverington Ave.
Manyunk
Philadelphia, PA
(215) 482-9004

Philadelphia Antique Center
126 Leverington Ave.
Manyunk
Philadelphia, PA
(215) 487-3467

Sandy Demaio Antique & Estate
  Jewelry
4359 Main St.
Manyunk
Philadelphia, PA
(215) 508-0200

The Furniture Workshop
Main St. & Green Lane
Manyunk
Philadelphia, PA
(215) 483-6160

Two By Four
3797 Main St.
Manyunk
Philadelphia, PA
(215) 482-9494

Uncle Shakey's Antiques & Restoration
102 Jamestown St. and
128 Leverington Ave.
Manyunk
Philadelphia, PA
(215) 482-7703

# Philadelphia's *Newest* Antique District

**❶ *John Dorety Antiques***
900 South St.
215-625-2728
20,000 sq. ft. of mantels, stained glass, iron, bars.
Mon-Sat 9-5, Sunday by chance.

**❷ *All Good Antiques***
620 S. Ninth St.
215-923-5291
Funky, Vintage & Antique, Funiture & Collectibles. It really is All Good!
Thurs-Sat 12-6, Sun 12-5 and by appt.

**❸ *South St. Jewelry Exchange***
648 South St.
215-925-9600
Buying and selling estate jewelry, coins, watches, sterling and diamonds.
Mon-Thur 11-6, Fri-Sat 11-7, Sun 12-6

**❹ *Anastacia's Antiques***
617 Bainbridge St.
215-928-9111
Victorian and estate furniture, lighting, jewelry, tiles and early photography.
Thurs-Sun 12-6:30

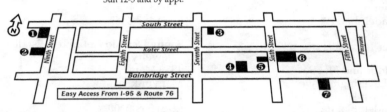

**❺ *The Den of Antiquities***
618 South 6th St.
215-592-8610
Fun furniture and curios from 1860-1960. World's Fair, Black Mem., Religious items.
Weekdays 1-6, Weekends 12-7

**❻ *South St. Antiques Market***
615 South 6th St.
215-592-0256
Center City's oldest indoor market, featuring 2 floors, 25 Dealers.
Wed-Thurs 12-7, Fri.- Sat 12-8, Sun 12-7

**❼ *Bainbridge Collectables***
514 Bainbridge St.
215-922-7761 Two floors, Victorian to Modern, 15 Dealers.
Wed-Sun 12-6 or by appointment.

## Philadelphia

Ad Lib Antiques & Interiors
918 Pine St.
Philadelphia, PA
(215) 627-5358

Aida's Antiques
615 S. 6th St.
Philadelphia, PA
(215) 922-7077
(15 dlrs.)

Alan's Antiques
413 S. 20th St.
Philadelphia, PA
(215) 545-6464

Albert Maranca Antiques
1100 Pine St.
Philadelphia, PA
(215) 925-8909

Alfred Bullard
1604 Pine St.
Philadelphia, PA
(215) 735-1870

All Good Antiques
620 S. 9th St.
Philadelphia, PA
(215) 923-5291

Anastacia's Antiques
617 Bainbridge St.
Philadelphia, PA
(215) 928-9111

Anthony Stuempfig Antiques
2213 St. James St.
Philadelphia, PA
(215) 561-7191

Antiques & Interiors
1010 Pine St.
Philadelphia, PA
(215) 925-8600

Antique Design
1016 Pine St.
Philadelphia, PA
(215) 629-1812

Antiquarian's Delight / Antique
 Market
615 S. 6th St.
Philadelphia, PA
(215) 592-0256

Antique Fair Inc.
2218 Market St.
Philadelphia, PA
(215) 563-3682

Antique Lighting
6350 Germantown Ave.
Philadelphia, PA
(215) 438-6350

Antique Showcase of Philadelphia
1625 Pine St.
Philadelphia, PA
(215) 545-0860

Architectural Antiques Exchange
715 N. 2nd St.
Philadelphia, PA
(215) 922-3669

au bon gout
1700 Locust St.
Philadelphia, PA
(215) 985-0783

Bainbridge Collectables
515 Bainbridge St.
Philadelphia, PA
(215) 922-7761
(15 dealers)

Bauman Rare Books
1215 Locust St.
Philadelphia, PA
(215) 546-6466

Barry S. Slosberg Inc.
2501 E. Ontario St.
Philadelphia, PA
(215) 425-7030
(Auctions every other Thurs.)

Belle Epoque Antiques
1029 Pine St.
Philadelphia, PA
(215) 351-5383

Bob Berman Antiques
136 North 2nd St.
Philadelphia, PA
(215) 482-8667 / (610) 566-1516
(By appointment)

Bob's Old Attic
6916 Torresdale Ave.
Philadelphia, PA
(215) 624-6382

Bobby J. Antiques
7th & Bainbridge Sts.
Philadelphia, PA
(215)922-7009

Calderwood Gallery
1427 Walnut St.
Philadelphia, PA
(215) 568-7475

Castor Furniture
6441 Castor Ave.
Philadelphia, PA
(215) 535-1500

Charles Neri
313 South St.
Philadelphia, PA
(215) 923-6669

Crossroads
2135 S. 61st St.
Philadephia, PA
(215) 726-1368

Dante's Furniture Refinishing
1631 Meadow St.
Philadelphia, PA
(215) 744-7345

David David Gallery
260 S. 18th St.
Philadelphia, PA
(215) 735-2922

DeHoogh Gallery
1624 Pine St.
Philadelphia, PA
(215) 735-7722

Delectable Collectibles
701 S. 61
Philadelphia, PA
(215) 471-6066
(By appointment only.)

DLT
1635 Germantown Ave.
Philadelphia, PA
(215) 769-0977

Dorety's
900 South St.
Philadelphia, PA
(215) 625-2728
(Antique architectural elements &
   furniture.)

Eberhardt's Antiques
2010 Walnut St.
Philadelphia, PA
(215) 568-1877
(Porcelain, china & orientalia)

Elena's Discoveries
509 S. 6th St.
Philadelphia, PA
(215) 925-0566

Estate Antique & Oriental Rug Gallery
1034 Pine St.
Philadelphia, PA
(215) 922-5714

Findings
246 Race St.
Philadelphia, PA
(215) 923-0988

First Loyalty Antiques
1036 Pine St.
Philadelphia, PA
(215) 592-1670

Freeman/ Fine Arts of Philadelphia
1808 Chestnut St.
Philadelphia, PA
(215) 563-9275
(Auctions every Wed, 10:00 am.)

G.B. Schaeffer Antiques
1014 Pine St.
Philadelphia, PA
(215) 923-2263

Gargoyles
512 South 3rd St.
Philadelphia, PA
(215) 629-1700

Glendora Byrd
5340 Germantown Ave.
Philadelphia, PA
(215) 843-4055

Gilbert's Upholstery
1627 Orthodox
Philadelphia, PA
(215) 744-5385

Graham Arader III
1308 Walnut St.
Philadelphia, PA
(215) 735-8811
(Antique prints)

Hampton Court
6th & Lombard Sts.
Philadelphia, PA
(215) 925-5321

Hotel Furniture Liquidations
5301 Tacony St. Bldg. 44
Philadelphia, PA
(215) 744-4645

I. Brewster & Co.
1628 Walnut St.
Philadelphia, PA
(215) 731-9200

Jack McGlinn Antiques
5314 Germantown Ave.
Philadelphia, PA
(215) 438-3766

Jansen Antiques
1042 Pine St.
Philadelphia, PA
(215) 922-5594

Jansen Antiques
262 S. 20th St.
Philadelphia, PA
(215) 592-6170

Jeffrey L. Biber
1030 Pine St.
Philadelphia, PA
(215) 574-3633

Jules Clock Shop
216 Market St.
Philadelphia, PA
(215) 922-3418

Kohn & Kohn Antiques
1112 Pine St.
Philadelphia, PA
(215) 923-0432

Lawndale Coin & Collectibles
6322 Rising Sun Ave.
Philadelphia, PA
(215) 745-8911

Liao Oriental Antiques
607-09 Bainbridge St.
Philadelphia, PA
(215) 574-9410

M. Finkel & Daughter
936 Pine St.
Philadelphia, PA
(215) 627-7797

Maggie's Drawers
706 S. 4th St.
Philadelphia, PA
(215) 923-5003

Mario's Antique Shop
1020 Pine St.
Philadelphia, PA
(215) 922-0230

Martha Hutchinson
10 E. Hartwell Lane
Philadelphia, PA
(215) 248-1326

Material Culture
4700 Wissahickon Ave.
Philadelphia, PA
(215) 849-8030

Maude's Curiosity Shop
6665 Germantown Ave.
Philadelphia, PA
(215) 438-1189

McCarty Antiques
7101 Emlen Rd.
Mt. Airy
Philadelphia, PA
(215) 247-7171

Metro Antiques
257 S. 20th St.
Philadelphia, PA
(215) 545-3555

Mode Moderne
159 N. 3rd St.
Philadelphia, PA
(215) 627-0299

Moderne Gallery
111 N. 3rd St.
Philadelphia, PA
(215) 923-8536

Newman Galleries
1625 Walnut St.
Philadelphia, PA
(215) 563-1779
(Art)

Niederkorn Antique Silver
200 S. Locust St.
Philadelphia, PA
(215) 567-2606

Olde City Antiques & Collectibles
33 S. 2nd St.
Philadelphia, PA
(215) 413-1944

Old Curiosity Shop
5338 Germantown Ave.
Philadelphia, PA
(215) 849-8508

Phila. Estate Liquidators
501 Fairmount Ave.
Philadelphia, PA
(215) 925-8690/(609) 541-4270

Philadelphia Trading Post
4021 Market St.
Philadelphia, PA
(215) 386-9855

Portobello Antiques
9 W. Highland Ave.
Philadelphia, PA
(215) 247-0181

Publick Antiques
6420 Rising Sun Ave.
Philadelphia, PA
(215) 342-5570

Quaker City Flea Market
Tacony & Comly Sts.
Philadelphia, PA
(215) 744-2022

Reese's Antiques
930 Pine St.
Philadelphia, PA
(215) 922-0796

Robinson Antiques
5320 Germantown Ave.
Philadelphia, PA
(215) 438-5780

Royale Court Antiques & Collectibles
 Ltd.
2024 Locust St.
Philadelphia, PA
(215) 893-3800

Schaffer Antiques
1032 Pine St.
Philadelphia, PA
(215) 923-2949

Scarlett's Closet
261 S. 17th St.
Philadelphia, PA
(215) 546-4020

Schwarz Gallery
1806 Chestnut St.
Philadelphia, PA
(215) 563-4887
(Art)

Sorger & Schwartz Antiques
1108 Pine St.
Philadelphia, PA
(215) 627-5259

South Street Antiques Market
615 South 6th St.
Philadelphia, PA
(215) 592-0256
(28 dealers)

Southwood House
1732 Pine St.
Philadelphia, PA
(215) 545-4076

Stuart's Stamps
1876 Cottman Ave.
Philadelphia, PA
(215) 335-0950

The Classic Lighting Emporium
62 N. 2nd St.
Philadelphia, PA
(215) 625-9552
(Classic & antique lighting)

The Den of Antiquities
618 S. 6th St.
Philadelphia, PA
(215) 592-8610

The Den of Antiquities Old City
16 3rd St.
Philadelphia, PA
(215) 592-8969

The Treasure Hunter
1614 Bethlehem Pike
Philadelphia, PA
(215) 233-4026

Thompson Antiques
Corner of 16th & Pine St.
Philadelphia, PA
(215) 545-1639

## Philadelphia (continued)

Thrift for AIDS
629-33 South St.
Philadelphia, PA
(215) 592-9014

Trading Post
4021 Market St.
Philadelphia, PA
(215) 222-1680

Trailer Park
1110 Pine St.
Philadelphia, PA
(215) 627-7275

Urban Artifacts
4700 Wissahickon Ave.
Philadelphia, PA
(215) 844-8330

Ursula Hobson
1602 Pine St.
Philadelphia, PA
(215) 546-7889
(Antique prints)

Vintiques on Kater
516 Kater St.
Philadelphia, PA
(215) 625-0705

Views of What Was
613 E. Passyunk Ave.
Philadelphia, PA
(215) 592-9191

Washington Square Gallery Ltd.
221 Chestnut St.
Philadelphia, PA
(215) 923-8873
(By appointment only.)

Watson 20th Century Antiques
307 Arch St.
Philadelphia, PA
(215) 923-2565

Yesteryear
6526 Rising Sun Ave.
Philadelphia, PA
(215) 342-9570